# SUPERNATURAL PROVISION

## Uncovering the Mystery of God's Blessing

DR. ED KING

Parsons Publishing House
Melbourne, Florida USA

Supernatural Provision—Uncovering the Mystery of God's Blessing
by Ed King

Parsons Publishing House
P. O. Box 410063
Melbourne, FL 32940 USA
www.ParsonsPublishingHouse.com
Info@ParsonsPublishingHouse.com


ISBN-13: 978-160273-154-7
ISBN-10: 160273154-3
Printed in the United States of America.
For World-Wide Distribution.

# TABLE OF CONTENTS

# 1

# The Promise of Provision

We are going to talk about the supernatural provisions God has provided for us. There are many places to go in Scripture where you can see God's hand supernaturally providing for His people. We will look at many healing miracles in the Bible, in addition to several other varieties.

Jesus walked on water and did many other miraculous things. He opened blind eyes, unstopped deaf ears, raised people from the dead; the list goes on and on. All those things are scriptural and need our attention. However, sometimes, we don't give enough recognition to God's supernatural provision where He meets the financial needs of His people. Sometimes, you'll have an event that doesn't seem to have economic implications on the surface, but it ultimately offsets a particular financial need. Therefore, it turns into a financial miracle. For example, Jesus' first miracle was when He turned water into wine at a wedding. On the surface, this doesn't sound like a financial miracle, but when you dig a little deeper, you realize that if you ran out of wine, you would have to dig into your pockets to buy more for your guests. So sometimes, God uses one avenue to offset a financial obligation.

God has ways of supernaturally meeting our needs. He is not necessarily going to float money down from heaven, so we are not talking about that. Instead, we are talking about things that have financial repercussions that can affect us in various ways.

## ABRAHAM'S PROVISION

We will look first at Abraham's provision because what God did with him was passed on to those who would come to God through Christ. This supernatural supply is at the core of many things you will see. It is not a financial miracle or blessing but a supernatural provision. In Genesis 22, God swore a covenant with Abraham, and several things took place in relation to that.

The events of Genesis 22 can be better understood if you understand types and shadows and grasp the background. When I say "type," I am talking about a biblical type that illustrates something else. An example of a **type** would be how the Holy Spirit is typified in the form of a dove. The Holy Spirit is not a dove, but He is typified as a dove. In another place, the Holy Spirit was likened to new wine when Jesus discussed putting new wine into old wineskins. So, the Holy Spirit, in one type, is a dove; in one type, He is new wine; in another place, He is typified as water when discussing the pouring out of the Holy Spirit. A **type** is something that represents something else. There are many biblical types.

Abraham made a covenant with God. It is important to understand that Jews are God's covenant people. Jews were the recipients of God's covenant with Abraham because they were his offspring. Therefore, the covenant God made with Abraham was passed on to the Jewish people.

We know the Bible records in Genesis 22:17 that God spoke to Abraham, basically saying, *"Your offspring will be as the sand that covers the seashore (earthly), but your offspring will also be as the stars (spiritual)."* Abraham has an earthly heritage in the Jewish race, and he also has a spiritual heritage—the Church—those spiritual babies born into the Kingdom. So, we become part of Abraham's covenant through the new birth.

Galatians 3:29 says, "And if ye be Christ's, then are ye Abraham's seed, and heirs according to the promise." The point being made here is that God required something of Abraham because He was making the initial covenant into which the Jewish nation and the Church would be grafted. This event is a crucial moment in time.

Abraham knew that Isaac was the seed through which the covenant would come. In other words, before this event happened, God showed him—by a dream, a vision, or some other way—and he had a knowing by the Holy Spirit that even if Isaac lost his life in this process, it wasn't permanent. That's important for you to know because you don't need to develop an incorrect idea about the God you serve. This event is first reported in Genesis 22, which says:

> And Abraham said unto his young men, Abide ye here with the ass; and **I and the lad will go yonder and worship, and come again to you**. And Abraham took the wood of the burnt offering, and laid it upon Isaac his son; and he took the fire in his hand, and a knife; and they went both of them together (Genesis 22:5-6, emphasis added).

God asked Abraham to sacrifice his son. When this event happened, Isaac was not an infant; he was a teenager. This point is critical. Without question, God did not want Isaac to be killed because he was the one through whom the covenant would flow. He was the one. Isaac was the offspring—a child of promise, and Abraham knew that.

Abraham launched out to obey God by offering up his son. Of course, he would have had great remorse like any parent in this situation, but there was something special going on in the process of this covenant. God is not going to ask us to sacrifice our children. This was a unique situation for one moment in time—for one reason and one reason only. The book of Hebrews explains it:

> By faith Abraham, when he was tried, offered up Isaac: and he that had received the promises offered up his only begotten son. Of whom it was said, That in Isaac shall thy seed be called: Accounting that God was able to raise him up, even from the dead; from whence also he received him in a figure (Hebrews 11:17-19).

Does the phraseology in that verse sound like something you recognize? Jesus was God's only begotten Son, and Abraham was asked to do the same thing God was willing to do. In a covenant, there is an exchange of promises, an exchange of tokens, an exchange of blessings, and there's also an exchange of curses. The wording is something like this: *If you obey me, these good things will come on you; if you disobey me, these bad things are going to come on you.* We don't like to talk about the curse, but the curse is out there if we disobey and don't follow on and follow through in our dealings with God. The results of

God's business with Abraham was passed on to those who would come to God through Christ.

## GOD WILL PROVIDE

We can see from the book of Hebrews that Abraham recognized Isaac as the seed through which the covenant would be established. Now, let's revisit Genesis 22 in context:

> And Abraham said unto his young men, Abide ye here with the ass; and I and the lad will go yonder and worship, and come again to you. And Abraham took the wood of the burnt offering, and laid it upon Isaac his son; and he took the fire in his hand, and a knife; and they went both of them together... And they came to the place which God had told him of; and Abraham built an altar there, and laid the wood in order, and bound Isaac his son, and laid him on the altar upon the wood. And Abraham stretched forth his hand, and took the knife to slay his son. And the angel of the Lord called unto him out of heaven, and said, Abraham, Abraham: and he said, Here am I. And he said, Lay not thine hand upon the lad, neither do thou any thing unto him: for now I know that thou fearest God, seeing thou hast not withheld thy son, thine only son from me. And Abraham lifted up his eyes, and looked, and behold behind him a ram caught in a thicket by his horns: and Abraham went and took the ram, and offered him up for a burnt offering in the stead of his son (Genesis 22:5-6, 9-13).

The next verse is significant:

> And Abraham called the name of that place **Jehovahjireh**: as it is said to this day, In the mount of the Lord it shall be seen (Genesis 22:14, emphasis added).

We will discuss verse 14 later, but I want to draw your attention to the name God used here. There are redemptive names of God: *Jehovah Nissi*, *Jehovah Tsidkenu*, and many others; these are redemptive names that illustrate certain qualities about God's character and nature. We often speak about *Jehovah Jireh*, and this verse is where the name originated. If you read this verse from the New Living Bible, it says:

> "Abraham named the place Yahweh–Yireh…" (Genesis 22:14, NLT).

The name used in the New Living Translation could be translated as *Jehovah Jireh*, which means the Lord will provide. So, when we use the phrase or the terminology *Jehovah Jireh*, that redemptive element of God's name, we're saying God will provide.

**As we talk about supernatural provision, we must first understand that God will provide.** Supernatural provision comes from the Lord. In the case of Abraham, he understood that God would provide a lamb as the sacrifice:

> "And Abraham said, My son, God will provide himself a lamb for a burnt offering: so they went both of them together" (Genesis 22:8).

In this verse is the word "lamb." Sometimes, the word "ram" may be used as an animal substitute for an offering. All the sacrifices of the Old Covenant, which used several different animals slain or offered on the altar of God, were types of the coming Christ. The Bible says that one sacrifice was made once and for all under the New Covenant. There are no more sacrifices to be made. So, this lamb or ram that God provided is a type of Christ.

**As we talk about supernatural provision, we must first understand that God will provide.**

Abraham took Isaac to the place of sacrifice to offer up his only begotten son with Sarah in a covenant exchange—a covenant between Abraham and God. In the covenant exchange, God required that Abraham put himself on the line so that in due time, God would be required to give His only begotten Son in like manner. This critical exchange is what enabled Calvary to take place. For that reason, this event was a one-time deal—one time only. God would never ask you to offer your child because you are not in a position like Abraham; even then, God stopped him and provided another sacrifice. It was a covenant exchange.

For this sacrifice, the Bible says Abraham and company went to a place God showed them. Remember, this was not, in actuality, the Holy Land at this time; the Jews had not inhabited it because the Jews or Israelites came after this event. There was not yet a land called Israel, so Abraham went to a place that would have been out in the wild—a wilderness. He went to a place that Scripture tells us is called Mount Moriah.

Some scholars believe Mount Moriah could also be called Mount Zion, located in Jerusalem today. The interesting thing about the location where Abraham offered up his son Isaac is that it is the same place God offered up His Son Jesus—the same exact location. Again, we must understand that the ram is a type of Christ.

**Abraham offered up his son Isaac is the same exact location where God offered up His Son Jesus.**

## BREAKING DOWN "SUPER" NATURAL

I spent a lot of time looking into this, and I hope to convey it with the same intensity that the Holy Spirit put in me. Words are important. It is essential that you diligently think about the words used in the Bible to understand what the Lord is saying. He's a God of words, as we see when we study His Word. Words matter to the Father. On the other side of the coin, words also matter to the devil because he is obligated to pay attention to your words and not cross the line of God's Word. Satan cannot operate outside the context of spoken words.

So, let's break it down a little bit. We're talking about supernatural provision. The word *supernatural* is obviously the combination of two words, *super* and *natural*. The prefix *super* means above, beyond, or over. For example, you use it when referring to your favorite superhero, Superman™, who is a super, over-and-above man. He's a man, but he's a remarkable man—super, over and above. He is not just any man; he's Superman™.

Today, we have all these different heroes with superpowers from which to choose. We see them in the movies, and they possess certain abilities you and I don't have. They can pick up buildings, fly at supersonic speeds, see through walls, and run faster than a speeding bullet. They have abilities to do certain things that average human beings can't do, so we say they have superpowers.

Another example is when we talk about a person with a lot of fame and fortune, and we call them a superstar. Certain athletes who excel in their sport begin to carry superstar monikers. They are stars in our eyes, and they are exceptional. They are players, but they're beyond the norm. It's good to be a player, but a super player would be a superstar. So, you get the idea.

We have superhighways that have vehicles traveling at high speeds in many lanes. Certain roads have become members of the Superhighway Club. There are also huge container or tanker ships that cross the oceans carrying vast quantities of oil, liquid gases, grains, automobiles, and the like. They call them supertankers or super-container ships. They are not average; they are super. I've visited the Panama Canal on a few occasions, and you can watch great ships pass through the locks as the water levels change to facilitate them. However, a supertanker is massive—the canal is not wide enough to accommodate one. It can welcome large vessels, but a supertanker is in a league all its own. Those gigantic ships must sail the long way around the southern tip of South America. They are exceptional—really BIG boats!

When discussing the prefix "super," it modifies something. The word "supernatural" certainly describes what is natural or according to nature. Humans have natural abilities; we can do certain things. But then there is something beyond, above, or over that natural ability.

You may have said, *"I've done all I can do. I've pushed myself as far as I can go."* Well, you need help, don't you? You need supernatural intervention—something beyond the natural. The Bible is replete with examples of supernatural provision; you see it repeatedly. This subject is where our study is taking us.

When we talk about supernatural provision, we are talking about provision from God that's beyond the norm. It is way outside the box—beyond what you could ever ask or think. The Lord works in the realm of doing supernatural things. We serve a supernatural God. He works in the natural world but is not limited to that natural realm. He is a supernatural God. There is such a thing as supernatural healing and supernatural blessing, and we are going to explore supernatural provision. We are talking about a God who meets our needs and is not limited to what the earth can do.

## I DIDN'T SEE THAT COMING

When God's supernatural provision comes, you might say, *"I didn't see that coming."* That's really the point with supernatural provision. I had an example of this recently happen to me when my cousin, whom I hadn't seen for many years, passed away. He never married or had children. He had no brothers or sisters, and his parents were dead; he had no immediate family. According to the state where he lived, his cousins became his heirs. Well, I didn't see that coming—somebody dies that I had not seen in over forty years and makes me his heir. When you divide it among all the cousins, it doesn't amount to an enormous amount, but it's more than I had when I started. I definitely didn't see that coming.

The purpose of this book is to build your faith because God will do exactly what He said He would do. He watches over His Word to perform it, and we are going to study His Word. As we talk about it, we will see it come to pass in our lives because the Bible is true. God wants to get something to you and not just by way of your standard ways and means—not just by your eight-to-five job working and slugging it out. He has ways of getting things to you that you can't even figure out. You go to bed and get up, and the seed springs and grows; you don't know how. You may not know how He will do it, but He will definitely do it. God's supernatural provision is above and beyond.

# 2
# Providence

Some circumstances can occur in life that you can't even fathom. You just never know. All money will do for you is give you options. It will provide you with life options. Do you need a car? Go buy it if you have the money. Do you need a house? You can have one if you have the money. You can be homeless and still be wealthy, but you don't have to be homeless. The subject of supernatural provision is much broader than money, but you can't leave it out of the equation.

When we hear the word "providence," we tend to think about divine intervention in the affairs of life. In other words, *"I see God's providential hand in this or that."* For example, there was a chance meeting at the mall where I ran into someone I hadn't seen in ten years, and a divine concept developed from that meeting. We might walk away from an event like that and use the word "providential" to describe the encounter. We could say the meeting was fortuitous. However, when you acknowledge the hand of God in what the world calls the coincidences of life, you begin to realize a providential God working on your behalf. God creating circumstances for your good.

Here's a Bible example: A man was on the back side of the desert tending sheep. Suddenly, a bush started burning intensely but was not consumed by the fire. The man turned to see what was happening with the bush. That man was Moses, and from that moment, the next 40 years of his life were entirely altered—completely changed. It was that providential event that changed his entire direction.

Again, we use the word *providential* or *providence* to signify that something is arranged, inspired, and originated from God. Providence rather than coincidence—I don't believe in coincidences. When we see the providential hand of God in something, it can change the direction of our lives.

The core or root of the word *providence* or *providential* is the word "provide." You can't even use these words without declaring that God is your provider. If you use "providential" without God providing something, you're in conflict with the word. It just doesn't fit.

If there is a providential event, such as in the case of Moses' burning bush, it goes without saying that God is moving in your life, and He will provide for you wherever He takes you. That's a fact. God is obligated to provide if He's the one who initiated the process. If you say an event is providential, that's what you are saying.

Therefore, if anything is providential, you are saying before you start on the journey that God will provide, or else you are in conflict with the word. If you don't believe God will provide, the core of the word "providential" doesn't even fit. Christians want to talk about God moving, or how God did something, or God initiated something, and then we actually worry about provision; we can't do that. If God initiated it, then God is obligated.

## WHERE GOD GUIDES

It's true that you must believe God for resources. However, it is a fact that you can't provide for where He's taking you. Once you are convinced God is taking you on this journey and that you can't provide for it, you better start trusting Him for your supply. Often, we think these are separate events: God leads you to do something, and then you must actively believe Him for the money. Yes, but if God leads you to do anything, He will provide. Like the tried-and-true aphorism declares, "Where God guides, He provides." That's the truth.

Someone complained, *"I thought God was leading me, but there was no provision."* That's a conflict of terms. Either you misheard Him, or you have messed this thing up. You either stepped outside His plan or failed to hear His plan.

Can you imagine Moses going down to Pharaoh, begging God for the money to get there? It should be a foregone conclusion that if God guides you, He will provide for you. But, we consider the plan and provision like two different events. I don't believe God leads you to do something, and then you run out of money—unless you messed up somehow.

How can you mess up God's provision? You may have accused Him of not meeting your needs, talked about how broke you are, or how God never does anything for you like He does for others. If you say things like that, you've messed up. It's time to close your mouth because the Bible says, "For out of the abundance of the heart the mouth speaks" (Luke 6:45). When you talk like that, your mouth predicts and prophesies your future. You conflict with yourself and the very concept of providence when you are in God's will and then beg Him for something.

**The will of God carries provision with it.**

So, the root of the word "providential" is "provide." It is impossible to speak of God's providence in your life without understanding His provision beforehand. You have to know that where God guides, He does provide. The will of God carries with it provision.

## PROVIDENCE WORKS BY FAITH

This all works by faith. You must have faith when you are in God's will, but now you know how to have it. In the end, it is God who meets your needs.

I remember years ago when God told us to go on television. You can't even imagine my argument against that! I could barely get up in the morning—could barely get across town financially—and God wants me to go on TV? I don't know how many years we've been doing it, but it's been a long time. The church has never missed one payment or even been late on one bill, and we won't. Why? Where God guides, He provides. Obey God's will with your life, and He will meet you when you do.

Someone might say, *"Well, we want it all done in advance."* It doesn't really take any faith to get your provision in advance. If you can see it all, why do you have to believe? Provision is when

God calls you and has already planned ahead to meet your needs. He already has it waiting.

So, the providence of God is the foreknowing and beneficent care and government of God. Divine direction, control, or guidance is the providence of God. It's the lot assigned to one by providence. In other words, God assigns you.

## DESTINY & PROVISION

I have heard people say, *"Your destiny is in your decisions. Your destiny follows your decisions."* Wrong. I don't care how much effort you put into your decisions and actions to be President of the United States; it probably isn't going to happen for you. I can get up one day and decide I am going to be an astronaut, but it's not going to happen. So, if you think your destiny is decided only by your decisions, you're kidding yourself. However, your destiny is determined by your decisions **in cooperation with the will of God.** You can decide not to do it, or you can choose to do it. Your decisions will carry you to your destination.

You certainly have a destiny, but you must cooperate with it through your decisions. Therefore, your decisions are not exclusively your destiny. However, what you decide will determine to a great extent where you end up or whether you obey.

God does have a destiny for you; He does have a plan for your life, which is providential. If God has a destiny for your life or a direction or a place He wants you to go, then it's an forgone conclusion that *Jehovah Jireh*, the Lord Our Provider, will provide. He provides what you need to get you to your destination.

When our kids were little, we played a video game with this little mountain climber who would run and jump. He would go down tubes and come out in caves, doing cool things that kept kids' attention. It was fun. This little guy would yodel and do all kinds of silly things. One of the things he'd do was go into a cave and come out with a bag of gold, and all the way through the game, he would collect bags of gold. In this game, this little man only had to have provision as he went.

Life in God is a lot like that video game. Are you going through life pulling a U-Haul™ trailer behind you? What do I mean? Well, you can't prepare for everything that's coming. You may get a BIG Swiss Army® knife that is two inches thick, with a magnifying glass, scissors, tweezers, toothpick, and cigar cutter. It has everything but a hairbrush, wheelbarrow, and table saw. But, regardless of how inclusive that Swiss Army® Knife is, you can't be prepared for everything. Those huge Swiss Army® knives are for the guy who doesn't know what's coming. You don't need to go through life with a U-Haul™ or a Swiss Army® knife as thick as a deli sandwich. You can't see all the future, and you don't know what's coming. Many of the things you plan for aren't going to happen anyway. So, you're making plans for no reason. The Bible says that as you go, God will provide. Everyone is wired a little differently. Some people need to plan, but some don't plan at all. Either way, God has promised to provide.

## GOD PROVIDES FOR ABRAHAM

With that said, let's return to Genesis 22:14, where Abraham named the place *Yahweh-Yireh, Jehovah Jireh,* which means the Lord will provide. To this day, people still call God that name. This is prophesied in Scripture, "...To this day, people still use that name as a proverb: 'On the mountain of the Lord it will be provided'" (Genesis 22:14, NLT). This statement is future tense. In other words, as you obey God with your life, He will provide for you.

The Bible says that God will provide as you go. We tend to let circumstances paralyze us to where we can't move. Someone says, *"Well, what if I buy a house and the housing market goes bad?"* Well, what if you don't buy a house and the housing market goes bad? You won't have a house either way. We are in a state of paralysis because we can't move. The lepers declared, "Why sit we here until we die?" (2 Kings 7:3). Sometimes, we just have to get up and do something. Make a move. Refuse to live in the paralysis of the moment or fear of the future. God tells us all the time, *"I am Jehovah Jireh, and I will provide."* I believe God would be much more pleased with us if we took some risks, and I'm not talking about foolishness.

**Receiving a higher limit on your credit card is not the Lord's provision.**

People believe all kinds of silly things about taking on a lot of debt. Someone says, *"Well, God sent me this credit application."* Receiving a higher limit on your credit card is not the Lord's provision, but many people believe it is. God gave them a better line of credit or someone who would co-sign a loan for them. No, that's silliness. People shouldn't co-sign for anyone or have someone co-sign for them; doing that is against the Bible.

Let's review Genesis 22:14 again, "On the mountain of the Lord it will be provided." Another way to say it is, *"In the will of God or the plan of God, all will be provided."* That's what it means. *Jehovah Jireh*—I am the Lord; I will provide. This verse says provision comes "on the mountain of the Lord," meaning in the will of God. They are one and the same.

**In the will of God, it will be provided.**

A person may say, *"Well, I can't do anything because I can't see how."* You must understand that you can't **ever** see how to do it. That's what faith is. Have you ever driven in the dark? Your headlights don't shine to your end destination. No, they just get you down to the corner. When you turn that corner, they get you to the next corner. You don't get all the revelation at once. You must put faith in the process. Revelation and provision come piece by piece.

If providence is God's divine intervention in human circumstances or God manifesting Himself or His will to us, it is understood that His provision is part of it. If God leads you to do something, He will provide for you. Underscore this in your mind because we seem to separate the two, thinking that when God leads me to do something, then I must believe Him for the resources. That's true, but your unbelief will not mess it up. If He led you to do it, the money has no choice but to show up. However, if you lead yourself to do it, you are on your own.

**If God led you to do something, the money has no choice but to show up.**

## THE DESIRES OF YOUR HEART

Let me clarify something here. If you want to do something, you should pray about doing it because sometimes God also gives us a will. Why did God say that He would give you the desires of your heart (Psalm 37:4)? He made that promise because He wants to do that for us. You do have some say, even in His provision. However, if God leads you, He will provide for you. If you want something just because you want it—and it's not sinful—my experience is that He will give you that, too.

Someone might say, *"You mean God will give me what I want?"* Well, the Lord is my shepherd; I shall not want. That's not a play on words. It's what He meant.

I've heard it said that God will only give what you need, not what you want. That's not even remotely true. God will provide what you need, but He won't give you anything if you don't ask Him. He said we have not because we ask not (James 4:3). So, if you want something from God, tell Him what you want.

If you say, *"Well, I don't think He'd give it to me,"* remember, faith is the only currency that heaven recognizes. Faith will go to God and extract anything it takes for this life. Anything. It doesn't matter what it is. The Bible says that as we seek God first, all these things are added to us.

> "But seek ye first the kingdom of God, and his righteousness; and all these things shall be added unto you" (Matthew 6:33).

## GOD'S TIMING FOR PROVISION

I wanted to examine the word "provision" and found some interesting information in my 20-volume dictionary; it's not in the three-dollar pocket version. A companion word to "provision" is the word "**pre**vision." It's a connected word that comes from the same root. The prefix "pre" means *before.* So, *prevision* or to *previde* means to prepare beforehand, to give it to you before you need it.

God knows you. He knows when you lie down and when you rise up. The Lord knows about you all the time. He's aware of what you will need years down the road. Why do you think the Scripture says to cast your bread on the water, for you shall find it after many days (Ecclesiastes 11:1)? You are sowing today for many days ahead. You are not just in emergency sowing mode.

If the rain flows into my yard just right, a patch of little mushrooms comes up. One day there aren't any, but the next day, there are ten mushrooms. Those things come up immediately. On the other hand, I have squirrels who like to plant nuts and seeds around my yard and in the mulch bed. But I have never seen a hickory nut or acorn come up overnight. Have you?

So, some seeds come up quickly, while others take much longer. Through that, God shows us He's planning for our long-term future, as well as planning for today. He is saying, *"I am working on a strategy for you that will meet your needs, not only today, tomorrow, and next week, but into your retirement years and beyond. I have enough to give to you and your children's children forever."*

## GOD'S POWER AT WORK

> According as his divine power hath given unto us all things that pertain unto life and godliness, through the knowledge of him that hath called us to glory and virtue: (2 Peter 1:3).

Do you remember the little man in the video game that I mentioned earlier? The little man went into the cave and carried out the gold. Most importantly, we have to realize that someone put the gold in the cave before he got there. So, the gold—our provision—had been given; it was there before we arrived.

This Scripture is written in the past tense. Let's look at it again, "According as his divine power **hath given** unto us all things that pertain unto life..." (2 Peter 1:3, emphasis added). That sounds like supernatural, divine provision for all things. That's as much supernatural provision as I can find anywhere in the Bible.

## WHAT DO YOU NEED FOR LIFE?

First, you didn't choose to be born, and you had no say in it. You were put on this planet, and you didn't get a vote to come. So, we could say that your life was providential. You didn't have anything to do with it, but you are here anyway. So, one could deduce that our lives are in every aspect providential—in the hands of God.

Knowing that your life is providential, and God has promised the provision (to provide) for the events He initiates, we can understand this verse. It is saying, *"According as His divine power hath given—already put in place, prepared ahead of time—unto us all things that pertain to your life."* It has already been provided. That is what God said! Everything you need as providential beings was put here by the hand of God. Nothing has been left out. He has given to us all things that pertain to life and godliness.

When you choose God and choose to live a godly life, He says it is a foregone conclusion that He will meet every need you will ever have. The Lord is saying:

> *Don't you ever doubt me on this. I will never leave you. I will never forsake you. I will go with you all the way, and I will be absolutely—beyond a shadow of a doubt—your supernatural Provider for the rest of your eternity. Forever. I will be your supernatural Provider, not just in the natural realm. I will give to you all things that pertain to your godly life.*

Read this verse from 2 Peter in the Amplified Translation:

> For His divine power has bestowed upon us all things that [are requisite and suited] to life and godliness, through the [full, personal] knowledge of Him Who called us by and to His own glory and excellence (virtue) (2 Peter 1:3, AMPC).

It says all things "requisite and suited to life and godliness," all things required for life. God says not to worry about a thing. He is telling us:

> *I've got it all covered. I've been ahead of you. I've been down this path before you. There's a bag of gold right down there. Go around the corner, and I'll show you where it is. Everything you need is there. Don't take that huge Swiss Army® knife with you; you don't need all those blades, screwdrivers, and magnifying lenses. Don't take the U-Haul™. I have it all planned, and it's there waiting on you.*

# 3
# PRIORITIES & PROVISION

To launch us forward into supernatural provision, let's look again at Genesis when Abraham took Isaac up the mountain to offer him as a sacrifice to the Lord—a part of the covenant exchange with God. Let's revisit this passage in ***The New Living Translation***:

> Some time later, God tested Abraham's faith. "Abraham!" God called. "Yes," he replied. "Here I am." Take your son, your only son—yes, Isaac, whom you love so much—and go to the land of Moriah. Go and sacrifice him as a burnt offering on one of the mountains, which I will show you." The next morning Abraham got up early. He saddled his donkey and took two of his servants with him, along with his son, Isaac. Then he chopped wood for a fire for a burnt offering and set out for the place God had told him about. On the third day of their journey, Abraham looked up and saw the place in the distance. "Stay here with the donkey," Abraham told the servants. "The boy and I will travel a little farther. We will worship there, and then we will come right back." So Abraham

> placed the wood for the burnt offering on Isaac's shoulders, while he himself carried the fire and the knife. As the two of them walked on together, Isaac turned to Abraham and said, "Father?" "Yes, my son?" Abraham replied. "We have the fire and the wood," the boy said, "but where is the sheep for the burnt offering?" "God will provide a sheep for the burnt offering, my son," Abraham answered. And they both walked on together. When they arrived at the place where God had told him to go, Abraham built an altar and arranged the wood on it. Then he tied his son, Isaac, and laid him on the altar on top of the wood. And Abraham picked up the knife to kill his son as a sacrifice. At that moment the angel of the Lord called to him from heaven, "Abraham! Abraham!" "Yes," Abraham replied. "Here I am!" "Don't lay a hand on the boy!" the angel said. "Do not hurt him in any way, for now I know that you truly fear God. You have not withheld from me even your son, your only son" (Genesis 22:1-12, NLT).

This exchange was a one-time, unique event for specific covenant reasons. I want to be clear about this because some people misunderstand and erroneously conclude that God may require or expect the same of them, but He won't. Some people say, *"God caused Abraham to offer up his son; He may want me to do the same thing with my child."* God will not do that. We need to understand this correctly.

We find in this passage that Abraham went to offer Isaac. On the way up the hill, Abraham told Isaac that God Himself would provide a lamb for the sacrifice. The word "provide" springs us into this whole teaching that we are doing on supernatural provision. God will provide. Abraham identified God as *Jehovah Jireh*, our Provider, on this mountain top. The Bible says, "And Abraham called the name of that place Jehovahjireh: as it is said to this day, In the mount of the Lord it shall be seen (Genesis 22:14).

## THE RACE OF LIFE

Let's look back at 2 Peter:

> By his divine power, God has given us everything we need for living a godly life. We have received all of this by coming to know him, the one who called us to himself by means of his marvelous glory and excellence (2 Peter 1:3, NLT).

"Hath" is a past tense word. God has already provided the things that pertain to your life. So, **prevision** was necessary to do that. He provided for your life in advance. You say, *"Well, why don't I have it?"* Because faith is the only currency that heaven recognizes. To have it, you must start believing in God's provision.

Look at this same verse from the Amplified Bible:

> For His divine power has bestowed upon us all things that [are requisite and suited] to life and godliness, through the [full, personal] knowledge of Him Who called us by and to His own glory and excellence (virtue) (2 Peter 1:3, AMPC).

God has given us everything required and suited for our lives. When God put you here, you were not an accident. There are many things about life that we cannot control. We may think we do, but the truth is that we only have control over very few. You do have some, but there are many things in life—maybe 80 percent—over which you have no control. Some examples are your IQ, skin color, parents, or the time and place you were born. There are a plethora of things about your life that you don't control.

Because He set us here, God knew we would be here at this moment. Someone might say, *"Well, it doesn't seem fair that some have more and some have less."* However, that is changeable. It would be best not to complain about what you don't have. All you can do is pick up where you are. This life we've been given is not to see who can accumulate the most stuff at the end because you're going to leave it all behind anyway.

This race of life that we run is to see what we can do with what we have been given. All of us start with something—some have been given more, some alternatively, less. Do you remember the five talents, the two talents, the one talent from the Bible? All of us have been given something, and it's what we do with what we've been given that counts. I am not accountable for what I don't have, but I am accountable for what I do have. You must evaluate your assets and discover yourself to find out what you have. You are a treasure chest but often don't know what's inside. If you don't know, you must find out.

There are things you don't know you are good at simply because you've never tried them. A person could counter, *"Well, I'm good at…"* Yes, but you may also be good at some other things if you try them. Also, there are things you think you're good at, but when you compare them to what you're exceptionally competent at, they turn out to be a complete waste of time. You may be a fair athlete, but you might be a better surgeon. **Don't spend time on what is secondary; spend your time on what will give you the best return—and it's you who has to discover what that is.** Sometimes, we waste our gifts and efforts because we don't assess ourselves properly.

## SEEK GOD FIRST

Our priorities will determine our provision. We find this principle in Matthew chapter 6 where Jesus talked about how God provides for the lilies and sparrows. He tells us the backstory before giving us a promise. Jesus said:

> Wherefore, if God so clothe the grass of the field, which to day is, and to morrow is cast into the oven, shall he not much more clothe you, O ye of little faith? (Matthew 6:30).

The Son of God asked if God clothed the grass of the field, how much more will He clothe us?

In the next verse, He goes on to say, "**Therefore** take no thought..." (Matthew 6:31a, emphasis added). The word *therefore* appears for a reason; it is a connecting word. It means: because of everything I've said up to this point—therefore. Jesus is saying, *"Therefore, you can conclude this because of what I just said."*

Let's continue on in that same verse, "Therefore take no thought, saying..." (Matthew 6:31a). So, we take thoughts by saying them.

Thoughts can come to you, but you don't own them until you speak them. **A thought is not a sin, but a wrong thought spoken or confessed or spoken aloud is a sin.** Many think it is wrong if a thought zips through your mind. No, it is wrong to think and dwell on it. Thoughts come, but you must reject the bad ones. How do you reject a thought? You dismiss a thought by speaking the opposite—verbalizing a good thought. The Bible says, "Let the weak say I am strong" (Joel 3:10). So, reject thoughts of weakness by saying you are strong. The poor should say, *"I am rich,"* to combat poverty. So, you reject one thought in favor of another. We call this process **renewing the mind**.

Let's look at this verse in context where we see Jesus saying:

> Therefore take no thought, saying, What shall we eat? or, What shall we drink? or Wherewithal shall we be clothed? (For after all these things do the Gentiles seek:) for your heavenly Father knoweth that ye have need of all these things (Matthew 6:31-32).

The word "wherewithal" is a money word. When reading through these words quickly, it doesn't seem like it, but it is. If you take someone out to eat and want to pay the bill, you must have the wherewithal—the substance, way, and means—the money. You must have the wherewithal to pay the bill. You can't have the wherewithal without substance.

The word "Gentile" means a person without a covenant. You **were** a Gentile, but when you came to Christ, you **became** a child of God. So, it's not just talking about Jews and Gentiles.

It's talking about the saved and the lost—covenant or without a covenant.

We sway in the breeze as we sing the old gospel song, *"He's all I need. He's all I need..."* Well, how come Jesus didn't know that? He said, *"I know you have need of all these things."* So, He recognized that we need things. Life is just that way; you need a number of things to live. Remember, this is a Bible statement: You need things. You need stuff. He said we need things to live, but then He told us how to get it.

The next verse begins with, "But seek ye first..." That means things should not be first in our lives. Stuff is definitely not first. What should we pursue first? Jesus told us when He said, "But seek ye first the kingdom of God..." (Matthew 6:33). We are to pursue God first.

## HOW TO SEEK GOD FIRST

Now, you could say much about the kingdom of God. Someone may reply, *"Well, I seek God."* Yes, but how do you seek Him first? There are many ways. You need to have a prayer life. That's for sure. You need to have a Bible life. Seeking the Kingdom and not doing what the Bible says is not truly seeking the Kingdom first.

One law of the Kingdom is whatsoever a man sows that shall he also reap. Jesus said we must know the law of sowing and reaping and how to extract the harvest into our lives. We can see it in Mark chapter 4:

> And he said, So is the kingdom of God, as if a man should cast seed into the ground; And

> should sleep, and rise night and day, and the seed should spring and grow up, he knoweth not how. For the earth bringeth forth fruit of herself; first the blade, then the ear, after that the full corn in the ear. But when the fruit is brought forth, immediately he putteth in the sickle, because the harvest is come (Mark 4:26-29).

You pray and read the Word, but then you must do what the Word says. So, to seek first the Kingdom is to do what the Kingdom requires. Again, the Bible says, "But seek ye first the kingdom of God, and his righteousness; and all these things shall be added unto you" (Matthew 6:33). Your priorities will go a long way in determining the provision. What you put first will determine what comes back to you.

Putting God third, fourth, fifth, tenth, or not including Him at all will determine your outcome. In Mark 4, Jesus talked about seedtime and harvest:

> The sower soweth the word... And these are they which are sown on good ground; such as hear the word, and receive it, and bring forth fruit, some thirtyfold, some sixty, and some an hundred (Mark 4:14, 20).

So, thirty, sixty, and hundredfold come into play after it gets to good ground. Then you say, *"Well, all good ground should produce a hundredfold."* Not really. Some good ground will produce thirty, some good ground will produce sixty, and some good ground will produce a hundred. What's the difference? Let's look at the next verse:

"And he said unto them, Is a candle brought to be put under a bushel, or under a bed? and not to be set on a candlestick?" (Mark 4:21).

The Bible says that the spirit of man is the candle of the Lord (Proverbs 20:27). When you talk about a candle, you are talking about the human spirit—the place where God shines His light. It goes on to say:

"For there is nothing hid, which shall not be manifested; neither was any thing kept secret, but that it should come abroad" (Mark 4:22).

Where is nothing hidden? In your spirit. There is nothing hidden that shall not be manifested. Matthew 12:34 says, "For **out of the abundance of the heart** the mouth speaketh" (emphasis added). In other words, what is in you will come out. This truth is all in connection with thirty, sixty, and a hundredfold from verse 14; the topic didn't change.

Let's look at Mark 4:22 again in different translations:

"There is nothing hidden that will not be made public. There is no secret that will not be well known" (Mark 4:22, CEV).

"Whatever is hidden away will be brought out into the open, and whatever is covered up will be uncovered" (Mark 4:22, GNT).

We see in this verse that the "coming abroad," as it says in the King James version, is what manifests or what is seen—the thirty, sixty, and hundredfold.

The next verse says:

> "If any man have ears to hear, let him hear" (Mark 4:23).

Everyone has ears, but it's not talking about those things on each side of your face. This comment refers to your spiritual ears; that's what the Lord is referencing. The spirit of man or the heart is the candle of the Lord. Do you have spiritual ears? Do you hear God speaking? That's spiritual ears. Continuing in this passage of Scripture:

> "And he said unto them, Take heed what ye hear: with what measure ye mete, it shall be measured to you…" (Mark 4:24a).

The amount of heart you put into it is the return you get on it. Same soil. Same seed. One produces a hundred, and one produces thirty. The amount of attention you give to it will determine whether the return will be thirty, sixty, or a hundredfold. Jesus said:

> "…and unto you that hear shall more be given" (Mark 4:24b).

More of what will be given? Thirty, sixty, and a hundredfold. When you think about that, I don't believe the Lord stops with a hundredfold. If you are at a hundredfold level and need more, it increases from there. Here is an illustration to show you there are no limits to this.

> "For he that hath, to him shall be given: and he that hath not, from him shall be taken even that which he hath" (Mark 4:25).

It says, "For he that hath..." There is no socialism here, folks. Someone might say, *"That's not fair. Aren't we supposed to take from the rich and give to the poor?"* Not so, according to this verse. Jesus said that if you are rich in Him, you have more coming. It seems you can't get too rich in God.

## WHEN GOD IS FIRST

The Lord says that when you seek the kingdom of God first—seeking is the amount of thought and attention you give to something—then all these things shall be added to you. Our priorities determine our provision. When He's first, provision comes. As we read earlier, He has provided us with everything pertaining to life (2 Peter 1:3).

However, if you are on the wrong course, you will not be able to find your stuff—those things pertaining to your life. God has a plan for your life; when you are off the path, He is not providing for the detour. The Lord has a track set for you to run, but you must get on the track to utilize the provision stations all along the way. Have you ever watched a marathon race? It seems the competitors run forever, but along the way, people provide them with sustenance by way of water or other liquids to keep them in top form and refreshed. If you get off the track, you won't find the water people; they are only on the course or track designated for the race. The water people won't be found off the course somewhere. You must be on the path to get the provision.

Why is this important? Why is priority essential to provision? We find the answer to this question in Matthew 6, where it says:

"For where your treasure is, there will your heart be also" (Matthew 6:21).

When you are off track, you won't get the provisions you need. You must keep your heart in line with God because your treasure could be described as those things in which you love to invest. Someone may say, *"Well, I love the Lord, but I never give anything to Him."* That kind of statement is a lie that seeks to deceive us because the truth is that you don't love Him. You love video games because you invest in them. You love clothes. You love going out to eat. You love going on vacation. You invest in all that. Our deception causes us to lie to ourselves or rationalize.

If you never give to God, you can't say with any certainty that you love Him because where your treasure is, there is your heart. Treasure becomes an expression of your heart. That's why the Lord said to seek first the Kingdom, and then these things will be added to you. If He gave you a bunch of stuff without you prioritizing Him, then your heart would be in the wrong place. So, He has promised to supply for us if we put Him first.

How do you put God first? You put His will first place in your life. Does He have a plan for my life? Of course, but you have to put Him first. I can't claim God's provision if I'm not doing what He told me to do. If He called me to preach and I declined, He would still love me, but my supply would be limited.

# 4
# God At Work

Earlier, we talked about the providence of His plan. The providential hand of God comes on our life, and inside that providential event, we experience *Jehovah Jireh*—I will provide. God says, *"I am your provision to do what I told you to do."*

Let's look at some illustrations from Scripture of God's supernatural provision.

## DIVINE SUPPLY FOR THE FISHERMEN

Here's a familiar story in Luke 5:

> And it came to pass, that, as the people pressed upon him to hear the word of God, he stood by the lake of Gennesaret, And saw two ships standing by the lake: but the fishermen were gone out of them, and were washing their nets. And he entered into one of the ships, which was Simon's and prayed him that he would thrust out a little from the land. And he sat down, and taught the people out of the ship (Luke 5:1-3).

So, Jesus borrowed the boat and pushed off a bit from the shore. He wanted to separate Himself from the crowd so everyone could see Him. When He was ready, He began to preach the Sermon on the Mount. After Jesus finished, the Bible says:

> "Now when he had left speaking, he said unto Simon, Launch out into the deep, and let down your nets for a draught" (Luke 5:4).

Simon allowed Jesus to use his boat. In return, Jesus told him where to get a "draught" or haul of fish. In a sense, Jesus is paying rent on the boat.

The Bible says, "The blessing of the Lord, it maketh rich, and he addeth no sorrow with it" (Proverbs 10:22). The word "sorrow" is a similar word to the word "toil." So, when the blessing of the Lord comes, He will add it to you without toil. These disciples had toiled all night and caught nothing. When the favor of God and the blessing of God comes on you, He removes the toil. When God cursed the ground because of Adam's sin, He was saying, *"The earth is going to produce thorns and thistles, and you must harvest by the sweat of your brow"* (Genesis 3:19). When Jesus took the crown of thorns on Him, He took the curse of toil away from us; He took the curse of labor with no profit.

We see Simon's response to Jesus' direction for where to fish:

> And Simon answering said unto him, Master, we have toiled all the night, and have taken nothing: nevertheless at thy word I will let down the net (Luke 5:5).

In other words, Simon was saying, *"I don't see how it will happen. This guy doesn't fish, but let's appease Him. We loaned Him our boat, so let's do what He says."* That was probably what was going on here.

> And when they had this done, they enclosed a great multitude of fishes: and their net brake. And they beckoned unto their partners, which were in the other ship, that they should come and help them. And they came, and filled both the ships, so that they began to sink. When Simon Peter saw it, he fell down at Jesus' knees, saying, Depart from me; for I am a sinful man, O Lord (Luke 5:6-8).

Peter belonged to a fishing syndicate of four: Peter, Andrew, James, and John. He didn't believe Jesus at first, but it appears conviction is setting in at this point.

> For he was astonished, and all that were with him, at the draught of the fishes which they had taken: And so was also James, and John, the sons of Zebedee, which were partners with Simon. And Jesus said unto Simon, Fear not; from henceforth thou shalt catch men. And when they had brought their ships to land, they forsook all, and followed him (Luke 5:9-11).

God told Simon Peter that from now on, he was going to catch men. However, Peter later says he is going back to fishing as seen in John chapter 21, "Simon Peter saith unto them, I go a fishing. They say unto him, We also go with thee. They went forth, and entered into a ship immediately; and that night they caught nothing" (John 21:3). In the Greek, it says, *"I'm going back to fishing."* In other words, Peter was finished with ministry; he was going back to being a fisherman. However, he was going broke trying to catch fish, then Jesus came, and they witnessed another miracle:

> But when the morning was now come, Jesus stood on the shore: but the disciples knew not that it was Jesus. Then Jesus saith unto them, Children, have ye any meat? They answered him, No. And he said unto them, Cast the net on the right side of the ship, and ye shall find. They cast therefore, and now they were not able to draw it for the multitude of fishes. Therefore that disciple whom Jesus loved saith unto Peter, It is the Lord. Now when Simon Peter heard that it was the Lord, he girt his fisher's coat unto him, (for he was naked,) and did cast himself into the sea. And the other disciples came in a little ship; (for they were not far from land, but as it were two hundred cubits,) dragging the net with fishes. As soon then as they were come to land, they saw a fire of coals there, and fish laid thereon, and bread. Jesus saith unto them, Bring of the fish which ye have now caught. Simon Peter went up, and drew the net to land full of great fishes, an hundred and fifty and three: and for all there were so many, yet was not the net broken Jesus saith unto them, Come and dine. And none of the disciples durst ask him, Who art thou? knowing that it was the Lord (John 21:4-12).

Again, Jesus made it clear that their provision is in God's will, not their prowess or human abilities. It was supernatural provision, far beyond a natural supply. It was a sign that they could trust God with their lives and futures.

## FAITH & DIVINE SUPPLY

Our next example of supernatural supply is found in another passage from the book of Luke:

> Then he called his twelve disciples together, and gave them power and authority over all devils, and to cure diseases. And he sent them to preach the kingdom of God, and to heal the sick. And he said unto them, Take nothing for your journey, neither staves, nor scrip, neither bread, neither money; neither have two coats apiece (Luke 9:1-3).

In other words, He was telling them to travel light—leave the U-Haul™ trailer home with your four-inch thick Swiss Army® knife and forty bags of groceries.

Jesus called His twelve disciples together and sent them out to preach and take nothing with them. This statement was the precursor to a divine supply or a supernatural provision lesson, and He wanted them to learn it. Jesus wanted them to see that He would faithfully provide for their needs.

The first element of God's provision is always seeking His Kingdom first—seek first, and then all things are added to us. God told them if they followed Him, He would be their divine supply. And we find Jesus referring to the same group in Luke 22:

> "And he said unto them, When I sent you without purse, and scrip, and shoes, lacked ye any thing? And they said, Nothing" (Luke 22:35).

The disciples took nothing on their travels. Jesus asked if they lacked anything, and they responded that they lacked nothing. All they could say was, *"We didn't need a thing. You did it all. As we went, You provided!"* God is a provider. Where God guides, He provides. When God tells you to do something, it includes His provision. Abraham said God would provide when He told him to take the boy up the hill. So, Abraham had confidence in God's provision.

You must build up your faith so you can believe that your life matters—it counts. God cares about everything that concerns you. He cares about every atom in your body and numbers the very hairs on your head. You are not different, and you are not the exception. You are exceptional to God because He loves you and counts you as the apple of His eye, but you are not exceptional because He left you out. He did not exclude you. This divine supply is meant for you. God's invitation to "whosoever will" (Mark 8:34) is a very personal statement to those of us who trust Him. God cares about you. He cares about your job; He cares about your career; He cares about what you drive, what you wear, and where you live. He cares for everything about you.

Some people just don't want to believe God will supply. They say:

- *"I don't believe God cares about where I live."*
- *"I don't believe God cares about where I work or what I wear."*
- *"I believe God can do this, but I don't believe He can do that."*

My reminder to those who say these things is: Be it unto you according as you have believed.

You must change that kind of thinking. Take no thought saying anything other than God is your provider. You must not say anything else. His name is *Jehovah Jireh*—the Almighty One. He is *El Shaddai*, not El Cheapo. You may feel that you've stretched yourself as far as you can go, but it's not far enough. Instead, start saying this:

> *I do believe God. I choose to believe. He does exceedingly above and beyond all I can ask or even think, and that is what I choose to believe. He is doing exceeding, abundantly beyond all I can ask or think. That's what I believe.*

Throughout my walk with God, I have never had Him get cheap with me. I've been cheap, but not the Lord. If there's something I want that I can't afford, I learned to say what the Terminator™ said, "I'll be back." I may not be able to afford you today, but I'll be back.

We don't need to be thinking in terms of lack. There is nothing too good for you; nothing is beyond your faith. Your faith will bring it to you. The amount of thought and meditation will determine whether your return is going to be thirty, sixty, or a hundredfold.

**The amount of thought and meditation you give something will determine whether your return will be thirtyfold, sixtyfold, or a hundredfold.**

Let's continue in Luke 22. Jesus said, "Then said he unto them, But now, he that hath a purse, let him take it, and likewise his scrip: and he that hath no sword, let him sell his garment, and buy one" (Luke 22:36).

Jesus said, *"I'll provide when you go."* But the point He makes in verse 36 is, *"You need to put forth your own effort into it. I don't want you to sit on the porch and wait until the checks come. I'm a supernatural Provider, but you do what you can, and I will do what you can't."*

This teaching will change your entire world. You're not here on your own; you have a provider. Jesus validated His promise by asking if the disciples had lacked anything on their journey. The promise of divine supply was verified. God did what He said. However, now He wanted them to do what they could, and He would do what they couldn't do.

## TAX MONEY SUPPLIED

Now, let's look at Matthew 17 and see what happened when they returned to Capernaum, where Jesus lived.

> And when they were come to Capernaum, they that received tribute money came to Peter, and said, Doth not your master pay tribute? He saith, Yes. And when he was come into the

> house, Jesus prevented him, saying, What thinkest thou, Simon? of whom doth the kings of the earth take custom or tribute? of their own children or of strangers? "Peter saith unto him, Of strangers. Jesus saith unto him, Then are the children free (Matthew 17:24-26).

Tribute is a stranger's tax, but Jesus lives here. He's not a stranger. There wasn't a tax for people who lived there. Jesus was saying, *"I shouldn't have to pay taxes. This is an unjust tax."* Jesus has no consciousness of lack. When you can turn water into wine and feed a multitude with a little boy's lunch, you can't be taxed and not receive God's benefit. He went on to say:

> Notwithstanding, lest we should offend them, go thou to the sea, and cast an hook, and take up **the fish that first cometh up**; and when thou hast opened his mouth, thou shalt find a piece of money: that take, and give unto them for me and thee (Matthew 17:27, emphasis added).

So, Jesus was saying, *"You go fishing, and there will be money in the mouth of the fish; it will be enough to pay both of our taxes."*

Notice that this verse says when "the first fish that cometh up." You can only have a first fish if you have more than one. So, pay the taxes, sell the rest of the fish, and enjoy the blessing.

God has the supernatural ability to provide for those who seek first His Kingdom. As we seek God first, all these things will be added to us—supernatural abundance. That's as supernatural as you can get when a fish brings you tax money!

# HOUSES & LANDS

Let's look at the book of Mark:

> Then Peter began to say unto him, Lo, we have left all, and have followed thee. And Jesus answered and said, Verily I say unto you, There is no man that hath left house, or brethren, or sisters, or father, or mother, or wife, or children, or lands, for my sake, and the gospel's," (Mark 10:28-29).

This passage shows that the disciples are seeking God's Kingdom first. They left all they had and followed Jesus. Then, Jesus answered by saying, "No man that hath left house..." referring to mankind, which includes women. It includes everyone who has left material things behind to follow God.

This exchange occurred at the moment Jesus called them to follow Him and become catchers of men instead of fish. The Lord identifies people who follow His command—those who call or listen to His voice and obey it. Then, He brings up the subject of houses. That's as material as you can get.

I believe God put that first because there will always be some super-spiritual person who comes and tells you that Jesus only meant spiritual things in this passage. No, the house he mentions has a roof, floor, walls, windows, doors, and a three-camel garage. Super spiritual interpretations of this passage say God will give you a big harvest of souls. Well, I do believe that, but this is not isolated to souls because He put houses first on the list. That's a material thing. He said:

> And Jesus answered and said, Verily I say unto you, There is no man that hath left house, or brethren, or sisters, or father, or mother, or wife, or children, or lands, for my sake, and the gospel's, But he shall receive an hundredfold now in this time, **houses**, and brethren, and sisters, and mothers, and children, and lands, with persecutions; and in the world to come eternal life (Mark 10:29-30, emphasis added).

Lands are a material thing. It could be the land you live on, or it could be the land of your birth. It could be your inherited location where you grew up, things that are important to you, and your heritage.

Jesus said if we leave "…lands, for my sake, and the gospel's" (Mark 10:29), we would receive a hundredfold. Someone might say, *"Well, I didn't get a hundredfold."* That person may be a thirtyfold person because of the amount of thought and attention they give to it, which determines whether it's thirty, sixty, or a hundred. If you don't believe this promise, you may get nothing if you are stony soil. Ouch! I didn't make this up; it's in the Book.

When do you receive these houses and lands? This verse says we receive these things "now in this time" (Mark 10:30). Does anyone know when now is? **NOW** faith is the substance of things hoped for. Now is right at this moment. You can't be now in a minute, and you can't be now a while ago. There is only one time to be now, and that's this second. So, He said:

> But he shall receive an hundredfold **now in this time**, houses, and brethren, and sisters, and

> mothers, and children, and lands, with persecutions;… (Mark 10:30, emphasis added).

The world won't like you for living like this. They will say, *"Oh, you're one of those prosperity preachers."* This is not just something we preach; it's something we live. I'd rather be a living witness than a testimony of what someone else had.

There is also an eternal side to this promise. This verse ends with Jesus saying, "…and in the world to come eternal life" (Mark 10:30). Not only will God pay you here, but He will also pay you there.

Jesus promised, "But many that are first shall be last; and the last first" (Mark 10:31). What does that mean? If you know how to use God's system and follow His Word, you can start at the bottom and go to the top. If you don't know how to work it, you can start at the top and go to the bottom. It's not God doing it; it's you seeking God's Kingdom first; as a result, all these things are added to you.

So, God has promised divine supply and supernatural provision. Not just barely making it, but a hundredfold harvest on Kingdom investment.

# 5
# GOD MAKES A DIFFERENCE

> Wherefore, if God so clothe the grass of the field, which to day is, and to morrow is cast into the oven, shall he not much more clothe you, O ye of little faith? Therefore take no thought, saying, What shall we eat? Or, What shall we drink? Or, Wherewithal shall we be clothed? (For after all these things do the Gentiles seek:) for your heavenly Father knoweth that ye have need of all these things. But seek ye first the kingdom of God, and his righteousness; and all these things shall be added unto you. Take therefore no thought for the morrow: for the morrow shall take thought for the things of itself. Sufficient unto the day is the evil thereof (Matthew 6:30-34).

In this passage, Jesus is talking to the Jewish people, but a more applicable interpretation of that phrase for us today would be people with a covenant. So, when He talks about the Gentiles, He's talking about people without a covenant, not just those who are not Jewish. Anyone not born of God by His Spirit would be a Gentile in our current vernacular.

In an earlier chapter, we discussed the priorities of the children of God. In other words, as you seek first (as you prioritize) the kingdom of God, then things will be added to you. The Bible says that God knows you need material items in order to live your life. You need clothing, food, shelter, transportation—you need all the things it takes to live the life you live. God knows that you need all these things.

Some people tell you, *"God is all I need."* If it's true that Jesus is all we need, how come **He** didn't know that? In fact, He said, I know you have need of all these things. Jesus knows you need things to live. Sometimes, we have a super-spiritual way of eliminating what God wants to do on our behalf because we over-spiritualize it to the point where we can't admit we need things.

However, Jesus tells us to prioritize His will, plan, and purpose over things we need in this life. We are not here for things; His will is why we're here, but He knows we need things to do what we are destined to do.

In the passage of Scripture at the beginning of this chapter, God said if we would seek His Kingdom first, then all these things would be added to us. When discussing supernatural provision, we are talking about what happens beyond the natural. We naturally endeavor to provide for ourselves, but then there is that supernatural element to the labor of our hands.

The Bible says God has anointed us to obtain or create wealth to establish His covenant (Deuteronomy 8:18). It is that anointing that destroys the yoke. God anoints us to acquire things (wealth) to establish His Kingdom and accomplish His work. It's amazing that we can multiply our lives through money. You can go around the world with money through missions and never leave home. You can start a missionary campaign in the Philippines or feed the hungry in Central America with your giving.

For example, I was talking to one of my good friends recently. He wanted to speak to me about some important issues pertaining to the Gospel as he and his wife are getting a little older. He said, *"Ed, I remember when I had small kids at home, and we didn't have any money. We could barely afford to feed them."* He wasn't talking about his ministry; he was talking about his personal life. My friend went on to say, *"But, currently, I have 250 children from a country in Central America that get up every morning and meet us for breakfast."* Every morning for the last ten years, he met those children for breakfast through his giving. There was a time when he couldn't afford to feed his own kids, but now he's feeding children around the world. That's how God can change things, and you can't do it without having financial resources.

## THE DIFFERENCE-MAKER

*Jehovah Jireh* is our difference-maker—the source of our lives. Let's look at Malachi chapter 3, the great chapter on tithing that still applies to New Testament believers, where God promises He will open the windows of heaven to us. In verse seven, God calls His people to return to Him, and they respond by asking, "How shall we return to you?" In other words, when a Christian returns to the Lord after being distanced from Him, we call that revival. When we pray for revival in the church, we're praying for a return to the right things. We were temporarily sidetracked, but now we've come into a place of revival. So, when we return to the Lord, we come back to Him in a special and meaningful way.

As the people tithe and return to God, His response is:

> Then shall ye return, and discern between the righteous and the wicked, between him that serveth God and him that serveth him not (Malachi 3:18).

In this process of returning to the Lord, God says He's going to use that as an illustration to the world of certain things. He said we return to Him through tithes and offerings. That's how we return to the Lord. The New Living Translation says it this way:

> "Then you will again see the difference between the righteous and the wicked, between those who serve God and those who do not" (Malachi 3:18, NLT).

God is the difference-maker. He is the one who says to the world:

> *Do it My way, and you'll walk in the fullness of life—the fullness of blessing. Do it the wrong way, and I will also show you where that gets you. I will show the difference between those who are mine, who do it the right way, and those who are not mine and do things the wrong way. I'm going to illustrate it to the world for anyone who is willing to look.*

I've been young, and now I'm getting older, but I have never seen the righteous forsaken nor His seed out begging for bread (Psalm 37:25). In my own life and those closest to me, it's evident that those who serve the Lord have the best lives by far. The Bible says, "The blessing of the Lord, it maketh rich, and he addeth no sorrow with it" (Proverbs 10:22). Therefore, much of the sorrow in life is there because we don't do things God's way; instead we go the way of the world.

**So much of the sorrow in life is there because we don't live life God's way.**

One of the best illustrations of this kind of life is the children of Israel. Look in Exodus:

> And I will sever in that day the land of Goshen, in which my people dwell, that no swarms of flies shall be there; to the end thou mayest know that I am the Lord in the midst of the earth. And I will put a division [or make a difference] between my people and thy people: to morrow shall this sign be (Exodus 8:22-23, emphasis added).

In other words, He even considers how many flies are involved. This gets down to the basics of life. God's provision affected things down to that level. There were other curses on the people who were not serving God; this is just one of them. The point here is not so much the flies but the difference between those with a covenant and those without. Those with a covenant are not the same. You are not just like everyone else; you are different. You serve a different Kingdom. There is another way of thinking—a different way of doing things. God is illustrating a point. In this case, He is saying, *"I will show a difference of where the flies happen to land."* That's significant!

I'm not trying to be unkind, but many things going on in cities around this nation—the infestation of disease and drugs, homelessness, filth, and squalor—are God demonstrating the difference between those who serve Him and those who don't. One might say, *"Well, these are just poor people."* No, a distinct difference exists between being poor and something else happening here. Watch the disease rate climb in areas with filth and squalor, just as in the Middle Ages. A society can't legalize everything that's sinful and get the blessings of God. These things are manifestations of the people who have rejected the God of the Bible. Jesus Christ is the answer to everything. It doesn't matter what it is. Jesus Christ is not **an** answer; He is **the** answer.

## THE LAMB

As the exodus of the children of Israel begins, it starts with some basic things. Look in Exodus:

> And they shall take of the blood, and strike it on the two side posts and on the upper door post of the houses, wherein they shall eat it (Exodus 12:7).

Israel was told to take the blood of a lamb and put it over the door lintel or doorpost, and it would become Passover blood. Sometimes, in Christian circles, you might hear the phrase, *"I plead the blood."* That's referencing the Passover blood, meaning, *"You can't cross here."* There is a "no trespassing" sign up here. You can't pass the bloodline.

In typology, this Passover blood represents the blood of Jesus Christ that flowed down from Calvary's cross. The Bible teaches that without the shedding of blood, there is no remission of sin. The apostle John said, "Behold the Lamb of God, which taketh away the sin of the world" (John 1:29). Jesus was the lamb slain before the foundation of the world. So, the Passover blood represents the slaying of Christ. Israel was looking ahead to Calvary because it hasn't happened yet; Christians are looking back on it. At this point in the book of Exodus, Israel is anticipating Calvary. Look at the following verse:

> "And they shall eat the flesh in that night, roast with fire, and unleavened bread; and with bitter herbs they shall eat it" (Exodus 12:8).

The Bible says that Israel ate the lamb. What do you think you do at communion when you break and eat the bread? You are eating the lamb. In relationship to this, the Bible says in Psalm 103 that there was not one feeble person among them. They came out of Egypt without even one person among them being sick because they ate the lamb. When you receive communion and symbolically eat the lamb by taking the bread, you acknowledge that His body was broken so yours wouldn't have to be. By the stripes laid on Jesus' back, we are healed. This is a type of the slaying of Christ—the broken body of Christ that brought healing into our lives. It brought the blood for the removal—the remission—of our sins, and it brought into our lives the body of Christ that was broken for our healing. God provided healing and health through the Lamb to both Israel and the Church.

# FINANCING THE JOURNEY

Let's look at how God provided for Israel when they left Egypt:

> And the children of Israel did according to the word of Moses; and they **borrowed** of the Egyptians jewels of silver, and jewels of gold, and raiment: And the Lord gave the people favour in the sight of the Egyptians, so that they **lent** unto them such things as they required. And they spoiled the Egyptians (Exodus 12:35-36, emphasis added).

When you see the words *borrowed* and *lent*, the first thing you possibly think of is a business transaction. It sounds like they took out a financial loan. However, reading it from the Amplified Classic gives you a better idea of the meaning here, which speaks of something different from borrowing.

> The Israelites did according to the word of Moses; and they [urgently] asked of the Egyptians jewels of silver and of gold, and clothing. The Lord gave the people favor in the sight of the Egyptians, so that they gave them what they asked. And they stripped the Egyptians [of those things] (Exodus 12:35-36, AMPC).

On the one hand, you have Egypt, the wealthiest nation on the planet of that era, and on the other, the children of Israel, who were the antithesis of that. After the plagues, the Egyptians said, *"Good riddance, get out of here,"* and gave their possessions to the people of God. Absolutely, this is supernatural provision!

The Egyptians gave God's people their things—jewels, silver, and gold. In Exodus 12:38, you see that they also gave Israel their livestock. As a result, Egypt has never again been the wealthiest nation on the planet. This event changed their entire future.

Isn't it amazing that after Israel received all these resources from the Egyptians, God sent them to the wilderness where there was no shopping mall? Nothing to buy. No Amazon Prime free shipping. They had nothing to buy, so they kept their money in their pockets. God took His people from captivity to their Promised Land, making them the wealthiest people on Earth. This was supernatural provision, and He did it in a day.

Someone might respond, *"Well, I don't see how that could happen for me."* I don't see how it could happen either, but we don't have to see how. The blessing of the Lord makes rich, and He adds no sorrow with it. It is the blessing that does it, not my or your abilities. We must put effort into it, and the blessing does the rest. In the end, we see that they came out healthy, and they came out rich. This is the blessing of the Lord—the supernatural provision of God. They came out physically whole and financially wealthy.

*Jehovah Jireh* gave God's people supernatural wealth. They got the gold, silver, jewels, and clothing. They took the clothes that were given to them; they didn't steal them. Scripture says their clothes and shoes did not wear out during their forty years in the wilderness. God is a supernatural Provider. He is the God who's more than enough—*Jehovah Jireh* God. If He could do it for them, He can do it for you.

# YOU CAN ONLY DO SO MUCH

Let's look at another passage in Exodus:

> And Moses said unto the people, Fear ye not, stand still, and see the salvation of the Lord, which he will show to you to day: for the Egyptians whom ye have seen to day, ye shall see them again no more for. The Lord shall fight for you, and ye shall hold your peace (Exodus 14:13-14).

God told Israel, *"The toil that you've labored under, you will see it no more after today. Today's the end of that. It's over today."* Someone says, *"Well, it might come back."* No. Once you defeat the devil, he's defeated. He might take you another way, but he's not taking you that way. That way's been defeated.

The battle is the Lord's, and the victory is mine. There is only so much you can do. It must be the God who is more than enough getting in your corner. It must be the God who knows how to win who gets involved with you.

You can do some good through human effort, but the Bible says except the Lord build a house, they that labor, labor in vain who build it (Psalm 127:1). So, you can build a house without His help, but you can't do it without a lot of trouble, trial, and difficulty. God wants to build your house if you do it His way. You must put human effort into it, but human effort alone will not get the job done. Then, God will do for you what you can't do for yourself.

# 6

# A High Hand

Let's look in Exodus:

> And the Lord hardened the heart of Pharaoh king of Egypt, and he pursued after the children of Israel: and the children of Israel went out with an high hand (Exodus 14:8).

Israel left Egypt with a "high hand." It didn't say they were barely making it. It didn't say they had just barely enough. God said, *"I'm going to take you to a place where you will go out with a high hand."* If you stretch your thoughts as far as you can, they still won't be far enough. He said that He would do "**exceeding abundantly** above all that we ask or think" (Ephesians 3:20, emphasis added). All you can ask or think is not high enough for what He will do for you. He's going to do MORE than you can do or dream up. You can't think high enough. Stretch yourself as far as possible, and then let God hook on from there because He's able.

What does a "high hand" look like? Well, when they dined on that Passover lamb—representing the body of the Lord Jesus—that was a high hand of healing. They left under the high hand of God's healing power. God doesn't just want you to be healed; He wants you to be healthy. He doesn't want you sick and then getting better; He wants you never to get sick. There was none feeble among the children of Israel after they left Egypt (Psalm 105:37).

One may say, *"Well, you just have to take it as it comes as you get older."* No, you don't take it as it comes. You're a covenant person—you're different. You're not like everyone else. God is the difference-maker. These are the differences between them and you. They can't do it, but you can because He's on your side.

There's an interesting passage in Exodus 15 when God says:

> And said, If thou wilt diligently hearken to the voice of the Lord thy God, and wilt do that which is right in his sight, and wilt give ear to his commandments, and keep all his statutes, I will **put** none of these diseases upon thee, which I have brought upon the Egyptians: for I am the Lord that healeth thee (Exodus 15:26, emphasis added).

This verse talks about seeking first the kingdom of God. A better translation for the word "put" used in this verse would be "permit." God will permit you to get sick, but that doesn't mean He causes it. He will permit anything you permit because the Bible says, "Whatever you bind on earth is bound in heaven, and whatever you loose on earth will be loosed in heaven" (Matthew 18:18). God set it up where you have to give it permission.

What does Exodus 15:26 indicate God will heal for you? Every disease—all diseases. He said, *"I'll redeem you from all of them."*

What does He mean? It means all of them. Is heart disease included? Yes. Is diabetes included? Yes. Arthritis and migraine headaches? Sinus infections? Yes. All of them. There's always someone who says, *"I don't know if God would do that for me."* Well, I'm sorry you don't know your covenant.

## WHAT DOES A HIGH HAND LOOK LIKE?

When the Bible says He led them out with a high hand, what would that look like in the wilderness? Let me just give you a few things:

**First,** He gave them a cloud by day and a pillar of fire by night. What does that mean? They had constant leading and protection. The Bible says that the pillar went both before and behind them. Do you remember when Pharaoh's army was in pursuit, pushing them into the Red Sea? It says the pillar behind them stopped that army. So, God, in His supernatural provision, doesn't just provide financial things for you; He also provides the protection you need to use and enjoy those things He gives you.

**Second,** we find that He made a path through the Red Sea. That path was not a small one-person trail through the woods suitable for meandering. It was a large path—a considerable path as large as a roadway. It was the Red Sea Interstate!

**Third,** the Bible says that God congealed the water. Think Jell-O®. That wall of water was congealed and held back to let them cross. I don't know how God did it, but He congealed the Red Sea and destroyed their enemies—the Egyptian army that pursued from their rear.

**Fourth**, they became thirsty as they traveled into and through the wilderness for a few days. They arrived at a place called *Marah*, where the water there was bitter or poisonous. God showed Moses a tree to put in the water, and it became sweet. God performed a miracle by making the bitter water sweet. He supernaturally filtered the undrinkable, non-potable water into a drinkable refreshment.

Their situation was compounded by not having food to eat. There were no convenience stores or fast-food restaurants anywhere. They were in the desert with no place to buy food and snacks. What did God do? The **fifth** thing God did was to rain down manna from heaven on them for 40 years! He fed them in the wilderness for 40 years. I'm talking about the God who supernaturally provides. When certain death was staring at them, God rained down manna from heaven.

When it looks like you're facing certain destruction, let the manna-making, covenant-keeping, healing-bringing Lamb of God get in your life because He's more than enough. He's the God that provided the manna from heaven. He's the God who provided water in the wilderness.

As they continued in the wilderness, they ran out of water again. The **sixth** thing God did was to tell Moses to strike the rock, and water flowed from it. They didn't camp out around the oasis at *Marah*; they stayed in motion, doing the will of God. Seek first the kingdom of God, and then these things will be added. So, as they moved forward, God supplied water from a rock.

Let me touch on something here. It was later when the children of Israel were again without water. God told Moses to speak to the rock the second time, but Moses struck it and got into trouble. God still brought water out of the rock for the people, but Moses was unable to enter the Promised Land because of his disobedience. The reason is the rock is a type of Jesus. He said of Himself, if we drink of this water, we will never thirst again. He is the rock, and He is the living water. These are types of the Christian covenant.

**Finally,** their shoes and clothes did not wear out, and no one was sick among them. Now, that is what happened out in the wilderness. Under normal circumstances, all the people are going to die. Without the hand of the Lord, these are dire straits. But, when Moses went to Pharaoh, he wasn't wringing his hands. No, he went and did what God told him to do, and God was there to meet his needs.

## HE'S A BIG GOD

Let's take a look at the scope and logistics of moving approximately three million people through the wilderness. These numbers have been around for some time; maybe you are familiar with them. According to the Quartermaster General of the U.S. Army, Moses would have needed 1500 tons of food (three million pounds) each day to sustain that many people. It would require two freight trains, each a mile long, to supply that much food daily. Three million pounds of food every day for forty years, totaling 43,800,000,000 pounds of food while they were in the wilderness.

Additionally, the people would need firewood to cook. It would have taken 4,000 tons of wood and a few more freight trains every day, each a mile long. Besides all that, they required water. If they only had enough to drink and wash a few dishes, it would take 11 million gallons a day. To supply such an enormous volume would require a daily supply that would require a freight train pulling 1800 miles of tank cars every single day. It's mind-boggling to get your head around these numbers.

Jesus reminded us to "consider the lilies of the field, how they grow: they neither toil nor spin" (Matthew 6:28). He also told us that a sparrow doesn't fall to the ground without the Father seeing it (Matthew 10:29). Do you think He won't take care of you? Oh, ye of little faith.

I'm talking about the supernatural covenant-keeping *Jehovah Jireh* God, who is more than enough. Nothing pushes His limits. Israel wanted to eat meat, so God put quail on the ground, measuring two cubits deep. He has the ability.

Furthermore, Israel had to cross the Red Sea. If they marched double file on a narrow path, the line would have been 800 miles long, requiring about 35 days and nights to pass through to the other side of the Sea. Thus, to cross over in only one night, according to the accounts of record, there had to have been a three-mile wide opening of the Red Sea so that they could walk 5,000 abreast.

I'm talking about the covenant-keeping God who's more than enough. The *Jehovah Jireh* of the Word of God, of whom Abraham said, "God will provide." Do you suppose Moses calculated all this out before he left Egypt? I think not. You see, Moses trusted God and believed in His promises, and as a result, God took care of all these details for him. Do you think the God who is more than enough can take care of your little situation? All God needs is for you to believe Him, trust Him, and obey Him. Seek Him first.

I've seen some disputations of this particular Bible event, saying that these are not exact numbers. I'm not a quartermaster, so I don't know. I've never figured it up because I've never had to feed three million people. But I will say that regardless of what it took, that's a good illustration of God being allowed to do what He does.

## THE TAKEAWAY

The children of Israel were healed, wealthy, blessed, and prosperous. They left Egypt with clothing that wouldn't wear out. The children of Israel didn't need a doctor on the journey, and no one had to carry a sack lunch. God provided for them every step of the way. So, what do we take away from these events?

First, **God's ability will meet the needs of His people.** These events are written as an example for us (1 Corinthians 10:11). God wants you to read this and be inspired and allow it to build faith in New Covenant believers. God's ability to meet your needs is encapsulated in all this. What else can we take away?

Not only does God have the ability, but **He has a willingness to meet your need.** It is not just that God can; it's God will. It is not enough to believe God can provide for you; we must believe He will. God is willing to meet your needs, and He's willing to do it supernaturally by whatever it takes.

Our church took on some new television ventures, and our staff was talking about the expense because it always takes money when you do these things. Scripture says in Ecclesiastes that money answers all things. After making this television commitment, we found that money kept showing up to pay for it, and you don't know how it happened. When you obey God, it shows up—supernatural provision.

What else do we take away? **God's abundant provision**. What He did for them, He will certainly do for you. You must believe that. These stories are given to illustrate to you who we serve and our relationship with Him. It is God's will to provide for you. Where He guides, He provides. That is what providence means. That is what provision is. We need to trust God's goodness.

You say, *"That was just for the children of Israel in a unique event."* Well, then Jesus went to Calvary for nothing. Because if they had a better covenant than you, then Jesus' death was in vain. However, that is not the case. The author of Hebrews says:

> But now hath he obtained a more excellent ministry, by how much also he is the mediator of **a better covenant**, which was established upon better promises (Hebrews 8:6, emphasis added).

Everything the children of Israel got, you get. Everything God promised them, He promises you, and then some. You don't come behind in any of it.

These are survival tips for an overnight stay in the desert. Sometimes, when the deserts of life begin circling, and you feel like you're in a lean place—you feel like you're in the spiritual wilderness—the God of the Bible will never leave you. He will never forsake you; He will go with you all the way. He will never walk away. He will never turn His back on you. He will always be there. The God of the Bible is the God who's more than enough.

# 7
# Miraculous Provision

Let's go over to the gospel of John. I would like us to spend a little time looking into the wedding in Cana. We hear it referred to quite often, but we will explore it a little deeper. This is a story about God's supernatural provision and care. Let's begin in John 2:

> And the third day there was a marriage in Cana of Galilee; and the mother of Jesus was there: And both Jesus was called, and his disciples, to the marriage. And when they wanted wine, the mother of Jesus saith unto him, they have no wine. Jesus saith unto her, Woman, what have I to do with thee? mine hour is not yet come. His mother saith unto the servants, Whatsoever he saith unto you, do it. And there were set there six waterpots of stone, after the manner of the purifying of the Jews, containing two or three firkins apiece. Jesus saith unto them, Fill the waterpots with water. And they filled them up to the brim. And he saith unto them, Draw out now, and bear unto the governor of the feast. And they bare it. When the ruler of the feast had tasted the water that was made wine,

> and knew not whence it was: (but the servants which drew the water knew;) the governor of the feast called the bridegroom. And saith unto him, Every man at the beginning doth set forth good wine; and when men have well drunk, then that which is worse: but thou hast kept the good wine until now. This beginning of miracles did Jesus in Cana of Galilee, and manifested forth his glory; and his disciples believed on him (John 2:1-11).

This is the record of Jesus' first miracle. Obviously, this is a story of supernatural provision, but there's a lot more to it—if you look past the surface.

Look at verse one. It says:

> "And the third day there was a marriage in Cana of Galilee…" (John 2:1).

This wedding wasn't like one that we might see today, where people spend an afternoon or evening in celebration. A traditional wedding today will generally be over in a day or two. However, the Jewish tradition of long ago was much different, and the wedding was much more festive than we usually see. What does the phrase "third day" mean in this verse? The third day from when? The third day of the week? Many people who read that verse believe it was the third day of the festivities because the wedding celebration could last a week or two. If that's the case, it requires us to look back at a couple of things.

## THE BACKSTORY

To understand the "third day," let's first look at the backstory in the verses preceding the wedding. In the first chapter of John, it says:

> The **next day** John seeth Jesus coming unto him, and saith, Behold the Lamb of God, which taketh away the sin of the world (John 1:29, emphasis added).

The event in this verse takes place when John the Baptist was baptizing Jesus in the River Jordan. His cousin John testified, "And I saw, and bare record that this is the Son of God" (John 1:34). He was declaring that Jesus was the Son of God even though He had not performed any miracles nor yet launched out into ministry. Let's continue:

> Again the **next day** after John stood, and two of his disciples; And looking upon Jesus as he walked, he saith, Behold the Lamb of God! And the two disciples heard him speak, and they followed Jesus (John 1:35-37, emphasis added).

This interaction occurred the day after Jesus was baptized, and John had two of his disciples with him. These two disciples now begin to follow Jesus. Let's read further:

> Then Jesus turned, and saw them following, and saith unto them, What seek ye? They said unto him, Rabbi, (which is to say, being interpreted,

> Master,) where dwellest thou? He saith unto them, Come and see. They came and saw where he dwelt, and abode with him that day: for it was about the tenth hour (John 1:38-39).

In other words, they asked Jesus, *"Where do you live? Where is your dwelling?"* They went to Jesus' house and stayed with Him the rest of that day. Jesus lived in Capernaum and was baptized earlier in the Jordan. The next verses say:

> One of the two which heard John speak, and followed him, was Andrew, Simon Peter's brother. He first findeth his own brother Simon, and saith unto him, We have found the Messias, which is, being interpreted, the Christ. And he brought him to Jesus… (John 1:40-42a).

One of the two disciples was Andrew, Simon Peter's brother, but we don't know the other's name. So, here we have one unnamed disciple, Andrew, and now we have Peter. There are three disciples following Jesus at this time.

> And he brought him to Jesus. And when Jesus beheld him, he said, Thou art Simon the son of Jona: thou shalt be called Cephas, which is by interpretation, A stone. **The day following** Jesus would go forth into Galilee, and findeth Philip, and saith unto him, Follow me (John 1:42-43, emphasis added).

To date, we have the day Jesus was baptized, the day they began to follow Him, and now we have the next day. There were now four traveling with Jesus: one unnamed, Andrew, Peter, and Philip. When these verses mention the disciples, it was not referencing the Twelve; this was before there were twelve. It was talking about this small group walking with Jesus here that goes to the wedding. This passage goes on to say:

> Now Philip was of Bethsaida, the city of Andrew and Peter. Philip findeth Nathanael, and saith unto him, We have found him, of whom Moses in the law, and the prophets, did write, Jesus of Nazareth, the son of Joseph. And Nathanael said unto him, Can there any good thing come out of Nazareth? Philip saith unto him, Come and see (John 1:44-46).

Now we have five in the group that was traveling with Jesus. The backstory to this miracle at Cana gives you a mindset of what's happening. Now, we go on to our target passage in John chapter 2.

> And the **third day** there was a marriage in Cana of Galilee; and the mother of Jesus was there: And both Jesus was called, and his disciples, to the marriage (John 2:1-2, emphasis added).

This passage begins on the third day of the feast. Scholars tell us that the journey from where Jesus was baptized to Cana of Galilee was likely a 20-hour walk. So, it possibly took them three days to get from the place of baptism to the wedding. So, they are into the third day of the feast, and Jesus is some 20 hours away on foot. He wasn't there for the beginning of the wedding festivities.

Have you ever been involved in planning, supervising, or presiding over a wedding? One of the biggest problems with a wedding is who is on the guest list—who we do or do not invite—and, as a result, who gets their feelings hurt and who doesn't. Now, the host of this wedding had a problem. Undoubtedly, Mary was originally invited, but now her son has come into town, and along the way, He picked up five more individuals. So, the host must have told her to bring them all.

There had to be thought that went into Jesus' being there. The host's mindset must have been, *"Oh, Mary, you have some friends with you; great, bring them, too."* He really can't say, *"Don't come."* You can see in the story that the host is having trouble with the guest list, and he doesn't want to hurt anyone's feelings. He's just inviting them all! Remember that this wedding is only on day three, with the possibility that it will run for at least a week. The host is setting themselves up to have a big problem!

Jesus was at the wedding because of His mother; the disciples were there because of Mary and Jesus. Next verse:

> "And when they wanted wine, the mother of Jesus saith unto him, They have no wine" (John 2:3).

Mary did not suggest anything; she just declared to Jesus that they were out of wine. Some propose that Mary meant they should leave because they were running out of refreshments for this big festive party. To save the host's family from any embarrassment, they were going to leave. Have you ever had a barbecue for a thousand people, and fifteen hundred showed up? You better have something in reserve in the back room. This is not good. Let's look at Jesus' response to Mary:

"Jesus saith unto her, Woman, what have I to do with thee? mine hour is not yet come" (John 2:4).

It was a significant thing when Jesus said the words in verse four. This wedding miracle is the first miracle Jesus had ever done; Mary had never seen Him perform a miracle, period.

It's important to remember that Jesus can only do what He sees the Father do (John 5:19). The one who determined when Jesus' hour would come was not Him or Mary. It had to be the Father who said it was time. In only a few verses, His hour was not here, and then suddenly, His hour came. It's important to understand that Jesus could not have done that miracle at the wedding unless the Father had willed it. To a great extent, I believe the Heavenly Father was endorsing Mary because of her statement. She couldn't request a miracle because she had never seen Jesus perform one; however, she knew He was unusual. Mary's reply to Jesus' rebuke was to tell the servants, "Whatsoever he saith unto you, do it" (John 2:5).

Mary had walked with Jesus and lived with Him since birth, and she knew if He said something, you better pay attention to it because it's coming to pass—it's going to happen. She knew that, but she had never seen Him do a miracle. This story is absolutely amazing to me!

> And there were set there six waterpots of stone, after the manner of the purifying of the Jews, containing two or three firkins apiece (John 2:6).

These stone waterpots are too heavy to move, so you can't just take them to the well; you must bring the water to them. The

Bible says the pots each weigh two or three firkins. ***Firkin*** is not commonly used; in Greek, it means “metretes,” carrying with it a capacity of 10.2 U.S. gallons. So, two or three firkins equal 20 to 30 gallons. It says six pots hold an average of 25 gallons per stone pot, totaling 150 gallons of water turned into wine.

When reading this story, we usually are awed by the fact that water miraculously becomes wine. We don’t often think about the financial miracle that took place. This may have been about a $12,000 miracle. Many scholars tell us that after everyone at the wedding party drank their fill, the excess could have provided a nice dowry for the bride. We tend to think about the water becoming wine, but we don’t consider God’s encompassing provision for that household.

Here is a family about to be embarrassed by not having enough for their big celebration. But suddenly, the tables turned. Now they have enough wine for the whole event and then some. I’m talking about supernatural provision. This is *Jehovah Jireh* provision at work—the God who will provide. I’m not teaching you about water and wine; I’m talking about the God who wants to meet your needs. “There is no restraint to the Lord to save by many or by few” (1 Samuel 14:6).

The host of the wedding was probably overextended and about to lose face in the community. This wedding was big enough to have a governor or ruler of the feast. The phrase “governor of the feast” or “ruler of the feast” actually means the keeper of the tables. For example, suppose you have a big party and don’t have enough tables to seat everyone at one time. Let’s just say you have 200 people and only three tables. You would have to eat in shifts with the governor of the feast watching after the event. They would be like a sophisticated wedding planner overseeing it.

Apparently, the governor of the feast didn't know they were out of wine because he commented that they had saved the best wine for last. Everyone's in the kitchen panicking, and the governor of the feast doesn't know it, but those who filled the pots were aware of the situation because they had to fill them up.

## NEVER ASHAMED

In light of this wedding miracle, look at Romans 10:11, which says, "...Whosoever believeth on him shall not be ashamed." The context of this Scripture is related to whosoever calls on the name of the Lord will be saved. When quoting this verse, we usually think about not being ashamed of Jesus in a public setting, and you should not be ashamed of Him in any way. The Bible says that if you are ashamed to confess Him before men, He would be ashamed to confess you before the Father and the angels. However, you can see this verse in the purest context when looking at different translations:

"'Anyone who believes in him will never be put to shame'" (Romans 10:11, NIV).

"'Anyone who trusts in him will never be disgraced'" (Romans 10:11, NLT).

> No man who believes in Him [who adheres to, relies on, and trusts in Him] will [ever] be put to shame or be disappointed (Romans 10:11, AMPC).

The concept here is that when we put faith in God, He does not want us to be shamed. The enemy wants to humiliate you. He tried to shame those people at the wedding.; he wanted to embarrass the family and put a stigma on the family that would stick with them. This event carried with it the family's prestige, and the enemy wanted to humiliate them.

However, God does not want us to be humiliated. He does not want you to be put to shame. Jesus was preventing the humiliation of that family, not just turning water into wine. Remember, everything in the Kingdom is a seed. So, the host's generosity was coming back to them thirty, sixty, and a hundredfold right then. The harvest on the seed was coming back right before their eyes.

The host probably had enough substance left over to pay for the event and probably would have a nice windfall. Everyone was blessed in the process. You can see the nature of Jesus here, and it's a great illustration of God's abundance. In the future, when you read about the wedding at Cana, you will see *Jehovah Jireh's* supernatural provision. Jesus' first miracle was a miracle of divine supply. His first miracle was a miracle that related directly to money. It had everything to do with money and provision.

## BUILDING OUR FAITH

If you see enough illustrations of God's provision, you might get to where you believe it could happen for you. It could happen. When you repeatedly see it in the Bible, there must be a "me, too" somewhere. It builds our faith because faith comes by hearing the Word.

There's another story in the book of Mark that we sometimes read too quickly. Let's look at the woman with the issue of blood:

> And a certain woman, which had an issue of blood twelve years, And had suffered many things of many physicians, and had spent all that she had, and was nothing bettered, but rather grew worse. When she had heard of Jesus, came in the press behind, and touched his garment. For she said, If I may touch but his clothes, I shall be whole. And straightway the fountain of her blood was dried up; and she felt in her body that she was healed of that plague. And Jesus, immediately knowing in himself that virtue had gone out of him, turned him about in the press, and said, Who touched my clothes? And his disciples said unto him, Thou seest the multitude thronging thee, and sayest thou, Who touched me? And he looked round about to see her that had done this thing. But the woman fearing and trembling, knowing what was done in her, came and fell down before him, and told him all the truth. And he said unto her, Daughter, thy faith hath made thee whole; go in peace, and be whole of thy plague (Mark 5:25-34).

Let's dissect this story a bit to emphasize a few things here. Usually, when we read this story, we are talking about the miracle power of Jesus and virtue going out of Him. The woman's faith pulled that *dunamis* power out of Him, and she was made whole. That's the essential part of this story, but sometimes, we look at the most important part and don't see the other underlying factors. That's a good story, but we want to look at a different aspect.

Mark 5:25 says the woman "…had suffered many things of many physicians, and had spent all that she had, and was nothing bettered, but rather grew worse." This woman endured this issue of blood for 12 years. She was unquestionably wealthy because she had enough money to go through 12 years of treatments from various physicians. So, this rich woman needs healing, but she is now broke because she spent all she had and had nothing else to give. She had come to the end of herself. Sometimes, God moves when we come to the end of ourselves. In verse 34, we read Jesus' response to her:

> "And he said unto her, Daughter, thy faith hath made thee whole; go in peace, and be whole of thy plague" (Mark 5:34).

There are three things mentioned here that are important to note as we look at this verse. If you pass by too quickly, you'll miss it. Jesus said to the woman with an issue of blood:

1. "...thy faith hath made thee **whole**"
2. "…go in ***peace***"
3. "…be **whole** of thy plague"

Starting with the last one **first**, Jesus said, "Be whole of thy plague," speaking about her physical healing. This word "whole" is obviously related to her healing. In Greek, "whole" is ***hugies,*** which is a word related to healing from disease. When He told her to be whole, He was talking about freedom from sickness and disease.

**Second,** Jesus said, "Thy faith hath made thee whole." He told her to be whole of her plague, but He also said her faith made her whole. In English translations, that word "whole" is the same word, but in Greek, it's a different word. Jesus says to the woman in this verse, *"Thy faith hath made thee whole (sozo); go in peace, and be whole (hugies) of thy plague."* This is a different word altogether. Now, ***sozo*** (pronounced *sodzo*) means to make whole, deliver, protect, preserve, cause to do well, make safe and sound, rescue from danger or destruction, and save from penalties of sin. That is a different word that has nothing to do with her sickness. That is a different wholeness. ***Sozo*** also carries with it much more than the idea of just being healed from your sickness; it speaks of completeness, in addition to deliverance from sickness. It's a complete wholeness—whole spirit, soul, and body. This woman was unclean and could have been stoned because she was in a crowd. She is physically ill, but she must have been damaged due to the social ramifications of being isolated from others. This word goes beyond just her physical body; every part of her is being made whole as a human being.

**Thirdly,** Jesus said, "Go in peace." Now, the word "peace" is another thing altogether that carries with it the idea of prosperity, quietness, and stillness. He was saying, *"I'm going to see to it that you get all the money back that you spent on doctors."* That's supernatural provision—provision beyond the norm. Those are the words of Jesus, not mine. For Jesus to restore this woman, He's not only talking about healing her body, but He's also talking about restoring her money back to her. This is a declaration of wealth. She was a wealthy woman and spent it all, and Jesus said, *"I'll give it back to you."*

The idea behind these three statements was to be ***whole of her plague***, **whole socially**, and **get her money back**. Christians are not just old pilgrims passing through the heat and the cold only to find God at the end of their journey. Let me share something with you: God is not waiting at the end; He is on the journey with you right this minute. God is right here right now. He's the God who's more than enough. He's *Jehovah Jireh*—the God of the right now. God is concerned about your healing, but He's concerned about your pocketbook, too.

Someone might say, *"Well, you shouldn't talk about that."* Yes, I should talk about it because people need to know it. The same God that gave this woman physical healing is the same God that said her faith would make her whole socially, emotionally, and in every other way where she's been damaged, and He also said her faith brings the peace of God that comes from His prosperity.

## THE SAME DEAL

What about Job? It's the same deal because He's the same God. He is the same yesterday, today, and forever. He never changes. He is the God who's more than enough. He's the *Jehovah Jireh* God, the Almighty—the "I will provide" God. He is capable of handling your situation. This woman spent all she had, and He declared, *"I'll be your supernatural Provider. I will be your supernatural provision."* Will He do any less for us? You find God's supernatural provision all through the Bible.

We read about the miracle of the water and the wine, and we don't see the financial windfall of what Jesus did for that family. When that host showed Him some kindness, Jesus didn't leave without paying. When you show Jesus kindness by seeking His

Kingdom first, He will pay His way. All He wants from you is for you to trust Him. That's all He wanted from that woman with the issue of blood. Jesus is saying to us, *"Trust me, and your faith will get it to you."*

The same God that provided for these people is the same God that will do it today. The same God that cared about them is the same God that cares about you. Repeat this declaration of faith:

> *My God cares for me, and He is concerned about me. He will meet my needs, but not just my needs. He is the God of more than enough—not barely enough; He is the God of abundance. My God is my source. My God is my supplier of whatever I need whenever I need it. He's more than enough. In Jesus' name, amen.*

# 8
# A Place Called There

When God presents a providential (divine, heaven-sent) intervention into your life, He has already underscored that He will provide for you. The Lord couldn't have an event that He initiates in your life where He doesn't provide. God has already given us—past tense—everything pertaining to living a godly life. Again, there's a past tense to God's provision.

Now, God doesn't provide for you so you can live a rebellious life. He provides for you to live a godly life, but we can still get off track. Even though God has a plan, we don't have to embrace that plan. We have some say in the decision-making. It is not automatic; it's cooperative. It takes both God and us to cooperate. You can't make Him do what He's not willing to do, but you do have to cooperate with His wishes. God has a plan for our lives, and we must cooperate with His plan.

## GOD PROVIDES "THERE"

There's an excellent account of the prophet Elijah in 1 Kings that you've probably read, but let's go through and dig into it a bit.

> And Elijah the Tishbite, who was of the inhabitants of Gilead, said unto Ahab, As the LORD God of Israel liveth, before whom I stand, there shall not be dew nor rain these years, but according to my word. And the word of the LORD came unto him, saying, Get thee hence, and turn thee eastward, and hide thyself by the brook Cherith, that is before Jordan. And it shall be, that thou shalt drink of the brook; and I have commanded the ravens to feed thee **there**. So he went and did according unto the word of the LORD: for he went and dwelt by the brook Cherith, that is before Jordan. And the ravens brought him bread and flesh in the morning, and bread and flesh in the evening; and he drank of the brook. And it came to pass after a while, that the brook dried up, because there had been no rain in the land (1 Kings 17:1-7, emphasis added).

In this passage, the prophet Elijah prophesied an unpleasant future for the inhabitants of the land. He said, *"You get no rain and no dew."* Well, the result will not only be a drought, but it also causes famine and everything that comes with it.

In 1 Kings 17:4, God tells Elijah that He "will feed Him there." God has a place called "there."

- "There" is in the plan of God.
- "There" is in obedience to the Word of God.
- "There" is found in the will of God.

It went according to Elijah's prophecy. Because he spoke a word that was unpleasant to the inhabitants of the land, he had to push himself away from public scrutiny. God told him to go and hide by the brook. In other words, he had to find a place of sequestration. He had to get away because he was most likely in danger for his life. It was not pleasant, but God protected him.

God's unfolding plan is not always easy. It's not sitting at home watching football on your 70" flatscreen television. He experienced some unpleasantness, but he was still in God's plan. The will of God is not always easy, but it is always the right thing to do. God promised us that when we do His will, He has already given us everything that pertains to that godly life.

God told Elijah to drink from the brook, and He would send ravens to feed him. The Lord put him in a place where he had water to drink—the nectar of life—during the drought. Elijah had water to sustain his life. Because he was in hiding, he couldn't go out and hunt or fish. So, God sent the ravens to feed him flesh and bread.

Elijah may have had a campfire of some type and cooked his food. He probably built a little comfort zone around him. If I thought there was even a possibility of being stuck in the wilderness, I'd take a tent. He didn't have access to a sporting goods store, but I'm sure he constructed a shelter of some kind while trying to be as comfortable as possible while stuck there.

## THE "THERE" ZONE

God fed Elijah "there." "There" is the place where God provides. To have the provision of the Lord, you must be in your "there" zone, and everyone has one. "There" is an interesting word. In Hebrew, it's the word ***"sham,"*** which has a three-fold application.

First, it has to do with **a place**—a place called "there." The definition includes the word *loco* in it—location. So, "there" carries with it the idea of a place. You can see from the story that there was a place Elijah had to go.

But if we look closer, we see that this word means more than location. The place called "there" carries with it a **timing component**—and timing has everything to do with God's provision. "There" has the impression not only of a place but also carries with it the idea of a time. You can be at the wrong place at the wrong time, or you can be at the right place at the wrong time and still miss what God wants to do. You have to be in the right place at the right time to be in the place called "there." There is more to it than just positioning. It also must be there at the right moment in time.

You could go to Azusa Street tomorrow and have a great historical tour of the place where that God-inspired moment in time when the Holy Spirit moved at the turn of the 20th century. However, you can go there and see where everything happened only in a purely historical context. If you weren't at Azusa Street when God moved, you were at the right place but at the wrong time. The great Azusa Street Revival has already happened. So, you're not going to experience that great move of God by going to Azusa Street tomorrow. You can go, but that doesn't mean you'll experience God's grand move like the people did years ago.

We tend to build shrines when we find ourselves at the right place. That's what an altar is. A great God-inspired event happened in the desert or wilderness, and people built an altar to commemorate what God did. Well, that's the place commemorating it, but it's not necessarily based on the time it happened. The time has passed. A lot of church tradition is based on place, but it's out of sequence. It's not in the time it happened. So, we build entire denominations, church traditions, and religious traditions, and we're walking out of sequence with where the Spirit of God is today.

We must find not only the right place but the right time, as well. What's God doing right now? But not what's He doing just anywhere and everywhere right now. What's God doing in me right now? There can be a move of God going on in a particular group of people, but if that's not where you're called to be, you must be with your people instead.

A person could say, *"Well, God wants me in a move of the Spirit."* That's how you get "Cruise-o-matic Christians;" they always look for God to do something. They run here and there, never put down roots, and never any benefit to the actual place where they were called.

The "there" zone is a place and time. However, there is also a third element in Elijah's story that has to do with a thing.

Let's look in Hosea, which says, "But they like men have transgressed the covenant: **there** have they dealt treacherously against me" (Hosea 6:7, emphasis added). Notice what it says: They transgressed the covenant, and they dealt treacherously with God. So, "there" had to do with a **thing**, and in this case, it was the covenant. In other words, "there" had to be related to a thing, connected to a place, and have something to do with timing. All those elements will need to be in your "there" zone.

Now, back to the story of Elijah. The Bible says, "And the word of the Lord came unto him, saying…" (1 Kings 17:2). What is the thing? The thing involved "there" is the word of the Lord. Israel had transgressed the covenant. "There" was in direct reference to the covenant and, in this case, the word of the Lord—God's instruction. You can be at the right place at the right time without it being God's will.

**Just because it's right for another, doesn't make it right for you.**

What is the word of the Lord to you? That instruction gives you your thing. Elijah obeyed the word of the Lord, so he obeyed the thing. He did not deal treacherously with the word of the Lord or the covenant, as it would have been the same thing. So, the thing in this case was the word of God.

Therefore, the timing for Elijah was now; it wasn't tomorrow, last week, a while ago, or sometime in the distant future. You could liken it to, *"You really need to go right now, or Ahab will take your head off."* So, we have the thing which is the word of the Lord. Elijah knew what to do. He knew the timing had to be now, and he had to know the place. God gave him the place when He said, *"I want you to go to the Brook Cherith."* So, there was a specific instruction from the Lord.

And so, your "there" always carries those ideas or concepts with it. First, the perfect will of God. What does God want you to do? The word of the Lord. What is the word of the Lord to you? What does God say for you to do? It is not the same instruction for everyone; it's not one size fits all. You are unique. He has a plan for you. God says, "I know the plans I have for you" (Jeremiah 29:11, NIV). So, there is a will of God for you.

The second element, again, to be in your "there" is to be in His timing. You may know God's will for your life, but you can mess it up and get ahead of God. If you don't believe that, ask Moses. At forty, he supposed Israel would know what he was called to do. So, Moses went to try to free the children of Israel, and it got him into a big mess that took him to the backside of the wilderness for forty more years. He knew what he was called to do; he just got ahead of the timing. So, there is a timing element involved. Just because God wants something for you—it may be legitimate, and it may really be God—but there is still a timing issue in order for it to happen.

What is the timing all about? There may be stuff that God must do to line up all the necessary things for you to do what you're supposed to do. People, circumstances, events, and many different factors could be involved.

Thirdly, you may know the word of the Lord and the timing, but you must put that with a place. Where does God want you to do it to be in His will and provision? God supernaturally provided for the prophet, but he had to be in a place called "there" before it could happen. **He had to be in the will of God, the timing of God, and in the place. It is no different with you.**

## HOW DO YOU KNOW YOU'RE IN THE "THERE" ZONE?

Sometimes, we want to tell God what He's supposed to do, but we need to allow Him to say what He wants us to do. We are here to serve Him, which means we obey Him.

In this place called "there" is where God provides. Actually, this is where supernatural provision is not only possible but is promised. It is absolutely supernatural for birds to feed you!! That is divine provision.

You may ask, *"Will God do that for me?"* If you are in a place called "there," He would. If you are just on a picnic on the side of a mountain, He won't. In that case, you need to run by the store before you go because that is not a place called "there." That is just something you're doing. Sometimes, we can be so casual with the will of God that it becomes just something we're doing, and then we wonder why there's no provision.

Someone else may ask, *"Why didn't God do that for me?"* Because you must be in a place called "there" before you see that. Ask me how I know.

I was listening to a great preacher with a tremendous worldwide ministry. What piqued my interest was hearing him talk about his television ministry. Everyone was ministering on television. All the influencers around him told him, *"You need to be on TV. You need to get this on TV. You need to be doing TV."* So, he listened, and he put a show on television. He said the problem was that it almost broke their ministry. So, he quit doing TV, and God's will and blessing began to flow back on his life. God's plan is not one size fits all. He had enough following to have his own television show, but it was not God's will for him. Just because you can doesn't mean you should. So, he had to correct the issue.

**Just because you can doesn't necessarily mean you should.**

When you correct things, it takes you back to the will of God. You put yourself back in a position of being in that place called "there." That's the sweet spot for the child of God. It's the place of God's provision, and the place where He shows His favor. It is the place where He brings His increase. It is the place where He showers His blessings. It is where He brings His peace, and we are led by that peace. If you're in a place without peace, you are not in a place called "there." It's a place flooded with His joy. If you don't have joy, you don't have strength. If you don't have any strength, you don't have endurance. If you don't have endurance, you can't make it. You must have joy for the journey.

If you are saying, *"I'm doing this, but it's just so hard, and I don't have any joy in it."* Then you are doing something wrong. You are either out of the will of God, or you are doing something wrong. If you have lost all joy in what you're doing, you're not doing it right.

## GOD SPEAKS TO YOU "THERE"

"There" is also the place where God speaks to us. If you can't hear the voice of the Lord, then you're not in a place called "there." Let me tell you how you start hearing the voice of God again: Get back to the place called "there." Go back to the spot where you got off track. If you're out of the will of God, go back to "there" to get back in it.

For Elijah, God provided food and water. The brook, however, did dry up. Sometimes, when the brook dries up, we just need to use more faith. But sometimes, when the brook dries up, it can be an instruction from the Lord. The Bible says, "And it came to pass after a while, that the brook dried up, because there had been no rain in the land. And the word of the Lord came unto him, saying..." (1 Kings 17:7-8). If you are led by dry brooks, you will be hopelessly misled.

Now, the dry brook is an indication that you should stop and listen. Here's a **nugget of wisdom**: The dry brook was not a word from God. The dry brook was probably an indication that God was getting ready to speak to him. So, dry brooks become signposts on the road to "there." That is your sweet place.

In this case, Elijah is at the brook, and God told him He would sustain him. I imagine some time had elapsed, and he had a nice campground to make himself comfortable. Chances are that he had settled in and didn't want to move. The point is that we tend to follow our human nature. We get comfortable in our setting and don't want to change it. By drying up the brook, God was stirring up his nest. Sometimes, you'll be fine doing something, but suddenly, you lose your joy, peace, and possibly your finances.

There are times when God may use a job for a season, but I'm not limited to that job. One job can serve you for a long time, but you don't work for a living. You work to have seed to sow. The seed is your living, not your job. God is your source. If He's changing the direction of your life, then you need to be willing to listen.

The thing in a place called "there" is the word of the Lord. So, there is a thing, there's a timing, and there's a place. It can be fine for a while; then, suddenly, you lose peace and favor. It used to pay you well, but now it doesn't pay you as well. The big commissions have dried up. Could there be a word from the Lord in that?

You don't work for a living.
You work so that you can have seed
to sow.

However, you can't spend your life chasing your discontentment. With that in mind, a dry brook is not a leading from God. It can be an indicator you need to get a leading from God. Sometimes, you just need to double down in your faith, sow a seed, and do the right things to get things moving again. Confess the Word. Do what you must do because the devil will fight your place of provision, but he can't beat you unless you let him.

## A PLACE OF CHANGE

Elijah, the prophet of God, is in a place of change, and the dry brook is an indicator for him to look for that change. However, you can't make a change without the word of the Lord. If the change is for change's sake, you are not being led by the Spirit but by the ring in your nose that the devil will pull to get you to go every way but the right way. I wish someone had told me this years ago. What a gold mine!

Let's read more about Elijah from 1 Kings:

> And the word of the Lord came unto him, saying, Arise, get thee to Zarephath, which belongeth to Zidon, and dwell there: behold, I have commanded a widow woman there to sustain thee. So he arose and went to Zarephath. And when he came to the gate of the city, behold, the widow woman was there gathering of sticks: and he called to her, and said, Fetch me, I pray thee, a little water in a vessel, that I may drink. And as she was going to fetch it, he called to her, and said, Bring me, I pray thee, a morsel of bread in thine hand.

> And she said, As the Lord thy God liveth, I have not a cake, but an handful of meal in a barrel, and a little oil in a cruse: and, behold, I am gathering two sticks, that I may go in and dress it for me and my son, that we may eat it, and die (1 Kings 17:8-12).

This woman was in a rough situation. Then God took the prophet with the anointing of supernatural provision on him and took it to that little woman who didn't have anything. It's the anointing that breaks the yoke (Isaiah 10:27), and Elijah had an anointing on his life to go in there and break that lack off of her. He could have stayed in his comfort zone and left that woman to die, or he could have taken the anointing on his life down there to meet her needs. God told Elijah, *"I have commanded her to supply you."* That doesn't go over well in the headlines today: *"Prophet takes all the money that the little widow woman had."* Another might say, *"Prophet took last morsel of bread from little widow woman."* However, those headlines don't understand that this was the hand of God moving the man of God to go to someone who needed supernatural provision. He had the anointing of supernatural supply, and she needed it. If anyone needed it, she did.

Elijah could have stayed at his campsite in his comfort zone, or he could have obeyed God by going down to deliver someone in need. Once he got there, his actions looked like anything but deliverance. When he got to her, God said, *"I told her to supply you."* Look at what Jesus said in Matthew:

> "Anyone who receives you receives me, and anyone who receives me receives the Father who

> sent me. If you receive a prophet as one who speaks for God, you will be given the same reward as a prophet. And if you receive righteous people because of their righteousness, you will be given a reward like theirs. If you receive a prophet as one who speaks for God, you will be given the same reward as a prophet. And if you receive righteous people because of their righteousness, you will be given a reward like theirs. And if you give even a cup of cold water to one of the least of my followers, you will surely be rewarded" (Matthew 10:40-42, NLT).

This passage in Matthew relates to what's going on here with Elijah. It was the Father who sent Jesus, and He also sent Elijah. This passage from 1 Kings shows the prophet going down to the widow woman. So, the prophet took his anointing down to her house to break hunger off that household. If she received him, it would bring supernatural provision to her house. The King James Version says, "He that receiveth a prophet in the name of a prophet shall receive a prophet's reward" (Matthew 10:41). It didn't look like supernatural provision when Elijah came and took from her. However, it was the supernatural providing hand of God moving in that little widow's life.

Elijah could have stayed up there by the brook, but the brook was no longer a place called "there" for him. His place called "there" was now with that little widow woman.

## BELIEVE GOD AND PROSPER

Let's look at 2 Chronicles in the King James Version:

> Believe in the Lord your God, so shall ye be established [stand firm]; believe his prophets, so shall ye prosper (2 Chronicles 20:20b, emphasis added).

In the New Living Translation, it says:

> Early the next morning the army of Judah went out into the wilderness of Tekoa. On the way Jehoshaphat stopped and said, "Listen to me, all you people of Judah and Jerusalem! **Believe in the Lord your God, and you will be able to stand firm. Believe in his prophets, and you will succeed**" (2 Chronicles 20:20, NLT, emphasis added).

The word "prosper" means supernatural provision. God was saying, *"If you believe His prophet, you will prosper."* He sent the prophet down to the widow woman so Elijah could break that curse off her house. Believe His prophet, and you prosper. What did Jesus say? Give a cup of cold water—give something to the prophet—and you will receive the same reward as the prophet. The prophet's mantle fell on the woman to make provision for her because God sent Elijah down there to her, and she cooperated with him.

The widow woman responded to Elijah as we can see in 1 Kings:

> But Elijah said to her, "Don't be afraid! Go ahead and do just what you've said, but make a little bread for me first. Then use what's left to prepare a meal for yourself and your son. For this is what the Lord, the God of Israel, says: There will always be flour and olive oil left in your containers until the time when the Lord sends rain and the crops grow again!" (1 Kings 17:13-14, NLT).

Since she responded to the prophet, God gave the widow enough to get through the day, and He also gave her enough until the famine was eradicated. Elijah pronounced that the cruse of oil would not dry up, and the barrel of meal would not fail through the whole famine because she cooperated with the supernatural provision of God in her life.

## NEW TESTAMENT ILLUSTRATION

I want to illustrate this a little more. We looked in the Old Testament, and we showed it to you through Jesus' words in the New Testament. However, we must remember that when Jesus ministered on this earth, He ministered as a prophet under the Old Covenant. Hence, the ministry of Jesus is still under the Old Covenant since He had not yet gone to Calvary and been raised from the dead. So, both of our examples are actually under the operation of the Old Testament.

Let's take our New Testament example from a story in Philippians. You'll be familiar with the passage:

> "But my God shall supply all your need
> according to his riches in glory by Christ Jesus"
> (Philippians 4:19).

Isn't that what the prophet told this widow woman? Is that not what Jesus told us when He talked about rendering to the prophet or the righteous man? Read this in context from the New Living:

> Even so, you have done well to share with me in my present difficulty. As you know, you Philippians were the only ones who gave me financial help when I first brought you the Good News and then traveled on from Macedonia. No other church did this. Even when I was in Thessalonica you sent help more than once. I don't say this because I want a gift from you. Rather, I want you to receive a reward for your kindness. At the moment I have all I need—and more! I am generously supplied with the gifts you sent me with Epaphroditus. They are a sweet-smelling sacrifice that is acceptable and pleasing to God. And this same God who takes care of me will supply all your needs from his glorious riches, which have been given to us in Christ Jesus (Philippians 4:14-19, NLT).

In this passage, we see that the Philippians gave financial help to Paul in his time of difficulty. He is talking about money here; the Bible says much about money. Paul wants the people to receive a reward for their giving. That's precisely why Elijah went down to the widow's house; her reward was for him to break the curse of death, break lack, and bring supernatural provision. Paul said, *"I don't need your money. I have enough."*

Sometimes, you hear people say, *"Well, you shouldn't be receiving an offering when you have all you need."* Really? What is the purpose of an offering? Is it so the man of God can get a payday, or is it to break the bondage of lack off the people? Which one is it?

Now, I want you to read this verse again as if you've never read it before:

> "But my God shall supply all your need
> according to his riches in glory by Christ Jesus"
> (Philippians 4:19).

King James Version is good, but the New Living says it so clearly that you can't mistake it:

> But this same God who takes care of me will supply all your needs from his glorious riches, which have been given to us in Christ Jesus (Philippians 4:19, NLT).

God is saying the reason for the anointing is to break lack off of your life—not so the man of God can get rich—but so you can have supernatural provision. That's the whole point. Paul was saying, *"I'm bringing this anointing to you to break the curse of poverty off your life now and forever. In the same exact way God has provided for me is the same way He will provide for you—believe His prophet, so shall you prosper."* When you obey the prophet, you buy into an anointing that will break lack off your life forever. We have gone into detail in these illustrations to tell you about a place called "there" and how to find it.

# 9

# Is Hard Work Always Enough?

The Bible is clear on the concept of work. In fact, you will find the idea of work—even hard work—prominently throughout the Bible. However, we will focus on Proverbs. Let's take a look:

> He becometh poor that dealeth with a slack hand: but the hand of the diligent maketh rich. He that gathereth in summer is a wise son: but he that sleepeth in harvest is a son that causeth shame (Proverbs 10:4-5).

So, the concept here is the act of working or not working can lead to blessing or poverty.

Proverbs 13 says, "The soul of the **sluggard** desireth, and hath nothing: but the soul of the diligent shall be made fat" (Proverbs 13:4, emphasis added). Years ago, the local newspaper had a comic strip called *"Nancy."* Nancy was a girl who had a boyfriend named Sluggo, short for sluggard because he was a little lazy. This verse says the soul of the sluggard "desireth and hath nothing." In other words, there are people who want things but will never get them because they are lazy. You will never get to where you want to be if you are lazy. You must work.

Look at Proverbs which says, "In all labour there is profit: but the talk of the lips tendeth only to penury" (Proverbs 14:23). In other words, just talking about something and not doing anything will lead to poverty. But through labor, we find ways of getting things done. I've found that when you're facing a task—especially one you don't want to do—beginning it is being half-finished. You have to start and break the inertia of inactivity. There are some things we just don't want to do, but dreading it won't bring you a return; you must begin the process.

2 Thessalonians says, "For even when we were with you, this we commanded you, that if any would not work, neither should he eat" (2 Thessalonians 3:10). The scriptural meaning is: If you don't work, you don't eat. In other words, especially in some sort of communal activity, a person who is not a contributor doesn't eat. If you're not making a contribution, you're not entitled to the benefit. You must be a contributor, and all of us can contribute something. So, we can see from the Bible that work—even hard work—is scriptural.

Then you come to the question: Is hard work always enough? If it was just hard work, would that be enough to get me where I need to be? Well, God wants you to work hard, but there is more.

## THE BLESSING AND CURSE

God created Adam and Eve and placed them on the planet in a garden. In Genesis, it says, "And the Lord God took the man, and put him into the garden of Eden to dress it and to keep it" (Genesis 2:15).

Adam's job under God was to dress the garden and keep it. The word "keep" also carries with it the idea of protection. He was to be a protector over what God gave him to steward. The garden was a specific location, and it was obviously a beautiful place. We know that Scripture calls it Eden, the garden **of** Eden or the garden **in** Eden.

I'm a warm weather person; I like the tropics. You can go to some of the most beautiful places in the world, but without people overseeing the grounds keeping the plants trimmed, pruned, and in order, even a beautiful place will become overgrown and corrupted by everyday living. I love Hawaii, and as beautiful as the islands are, they will go downhill in a hurry if they are not cared for and cultivated.

So, when the Bible says that God gave Adam the task to dress and keep the garden, that's what he was supposed to do. Adam wasn't just a weed-puller in the garden because weeds hadn't come into the garden yet. He was supposed to keep that garden in the order that God intended it to be.

Look in Genesis 1:28:

> **And God blessed them**, and God said unto them, Be fruitful, and multiply, and replenish the earth, and subdue it: and have dominion over the fish of the sea, and over the fowl of the air, and over every living thing that moveth upon the earth (Genesis 1:28, emphasis added).

When God gave Adam his assignment in the beginning, He blessed him in doing that assignment. So, Adam was doing what he did under God's blessing or with God's blessing on his life. It wasn't just hard work; it was work with purpose and work with a blessing. The point I want to make is what Adam did was done with the blessing and favor of God on him.

Those previous passages we looked at were before sin entered the world. After satan tempted Eve and they ate of the fruit, we come to our next passage in Genesis 3:

> And unto Adam he said, Because thou hast hearkened unto the voice of thy wife, and hast eaten of the tree, of which I commanded thee, saying, Thou shalt not eat of it: **cursed** is the ground for thy sake; in sorrow shalt thou eat of it all the days of thy life; Thorns also and thistles shall it bring forth to thee; and thou shalt eat the herb of the field; In the sweat of thy face shalt thou eat bread, till thou return unto the ground; for out of it wast thou taken: for dust thou art, and unto dust shalt thou return (Genesis 3:17-19, emphasis added).

In these passages, we have gone from the blessing to the curse. The curse was the result of sin. So, we had the blessing that brought the favor of God in the labor of Adam's hand and all that he was put there to keep and dress. Now, we have transitioned over to the earth operating under a curse.

We clearly see that there was a man and woman with the blessing of God on them to do the work, finish the assignment, or fulfill the mission that God had given them. However, once sin entered, the curse began to restrain and restrict them. We can see that it went from the blessing and favor of God on the laborer's hand to the curse of producing by the sweat of their brow. Now, they have to weed out the thorns and thistles. If you have it the way you want it, you must work by the sweat of your brow to get it. It's just not going to produce for you the way it was.

So, the blessing and the curse made all the difference. If it were simply hard work, anyone willing to work hard would be well-off. But it's more than hard work. There is a blessing on our labor, or there can be a curse on our labor.

## A SIDE THOUGHT

An interesting side thought comes from the verse we just read. God said:

> In the sweat of thy face shalt thou eat bread, till thou return unto the ground; for out of it wast thou taken: for **dust** thou art, and unto dust shalt thou return (Genesis 3:19, emphasis added).

Underscore in your thinking the word "dust." This verse says man was made from the dust of the earth, and we know that.

> And the Lord God said unto the serpent, Because thou hast done this, thou art cursed above all cattle, and above every beast of the field; upon thy belly **shalt thou go and dust shalt thou eat** all the days of thy life: (Genesis 3:14, emphasis added).

This serpent was a manifestation of satan. He beguiled Eve, and they partook of the forbidden fruit. Most people think the serpent is a snake because this verse says he would be on his belly or crawl.

Sometimes, we skip through the part about eating dust. However, the Bible doesn't just use words to use words; it uses specific words for a reason. Satan is the dust-eater. So, the dust-eater does not just eat the dust of the ground, but man is also dust, as we read in Genesis 3:19. Satan is the man-eater.

You can see the exact same principle in 1 Peter, where it says, "Be sober, be vigilant; because your adversary the devil, as a roaring lion, walketh about, **seeking whom he may devour:**" (1 Peter 5:8, emphasis added). That's a manifestation of the dust-eater, just with different terminology. The enmity between satan and man was spoken of immediately when sin took place, and the conflict remains today.

Satan still seeks to destroy you, and you won't keep him at bay if you don't know that. He's not your friend or your ally. The devil does not want to give you a flat tire or a bad day; he desires to destroy and annihilate you. If you play with him, he will kill you. It's like the song goes, "Don't dance with the devil; he'll make a fool out of you" (Phil Driscoll, 2011). And he will.

The dust-eater is the one who desires to destroy our lives. Those verses are prophetic in nature. That's just a little side thought that I wanted to share with you.

## TOIL AND WORK

I want to focus on another verse in Genesis chapter three. This verse is talking about when the curse came. It says, "Thorns also and thistles shall it bring forth to thee…" (Genesis 3:18).

It's important to note that thorns and thistles came with the curse. Again, the Bible does not casually use words. Various words are symbolic throughout the Bible. If you understand symbolism, you will discern more about Scripture and have a great depth of understanding.

Later in Genesis, not long after the effects of the initial sin began to be felt and the curse began to fall, it says:

> And he called his name Noah, saying, This same shall comfort us concerning our work and **toil** of our hands, because of **the ground which the Lord hath cursed** (Genesis 5:29, emphasis added).

Notice this verse says that because there's a curse on the ground, we must toil with our hands. Toil was not what was originally intended and was not evident until the curse was on the ground. Adam and Eve had a mission to keep and dress the garden; it was their calling and life's work. They had a fulfilling career because it wasn't burdened down with toil. Man was not designed to live in, live with, or live under grinding toil.

The whole concept of toil is to work with limited yield or to work and labor with diminished harvest—to work and labor where you can't get all you need. Toil has to do with the idea of scarcity. It has to do with the idea of not having enough. It has the idea that no matter how hard you work, you will come up a little short. We toil, and toil, and toil because of the curse on the ground. But work and toil are not precisely the same.

Work is a fulfilling commission by God to do a task. The Bible says, "I will satisfy you with long life" (Psalm 91:16). To be satisfied with a long life is to find fulfillment in what you do without dreading it. But when we toil, we dread it; we hate it, and then it doesn't even produce all we want. It's not fulfilling. We don't find peace and joy in the process.

God wants you to find peace and joy while you work. He doesn't want you to toil throughout your life. Toil is a part of life, but it doesn't need to be a part of your life; it is the lack of blessing on our labor. Laboring without blessing produces a life of toil.

Before sin entered and the curse came, God blessed the ground for the sake of Adam and Eve. He blessed what they did. Everything they did was successful. However, after sin and the curse entered, things they did somewhat worked, but there was always a fight to it. They were constantly pushing against the wind—paddling upstream—with no help from the environment.

Let's look at Matthew 6:

> Which of you by taking thought can add one cubit unto his stature? And why take ye thought for raiment? Consider the lilies of the field, how they grow; they toil not, neither do they spin: And yet I say unto you, That even Solomon in all his glory was not arrayed like one of these. Wherefore, if God so clothe the grass of the field, which to day is, and to morrow is cast into the oven, shall he not much more clothe you, O ye of little faith? (Matthew 6:27-30).

Jesus gave us this passage, but we don't always take the time to read it carefully. These verses come right before Jesus told us to seek His Kingdom first and all things would be added to us. In this passage, He gives a comparison of us to the flowers. He was saying, *"The lilies don't toil. What do you think you are going to get by toiling?"* Do you think toil is the answer? Do you believe hard work only is enough? Hard work without the blessing will not bear the intended fruit.

People spend their whole lives pushing things uphill. But so many people are trying to kick a dead horse and get out of a hole they are digging themselves. Life is not favoring them. Life is not blessing them. Life is not doing for them what it ought to be doing, and they know it but keep doing the same old thing. Working without the blessing. Laboring without the favor. Trying just to make it. If the horse is dead, dismount; get off of it. If you find yourself digging a hole, quit digging. Stubbornness and determination are totally different. I've been both of these things—most of us have. **Determination** is when you push through difficulty. **Stubbornness** is when you're too dumb to quit. But, sometimes, these two things look the same. You don't want to be stubborn, especially when things aren't working.

Referring back to the lilies of the field, they don't toil, and they don't spin. Jesus is giving us an illustration by saying, *"I don't want you to spend your life working without the blessing. I desire for the wind to catch your back. I want to put some wind in your sails. I want to do something for you that you can't do for yourself. I want to arrange some connections and favors. I want to arrange some events you can't do alone. I want to take you to the next level and the next place."*

## SEEDTIME & HARVEST

Again, I don't think words are in the Bible by accident. I believe they are chosen for specific reasons. Look at the parable of the sower in Mark chapter four:

> The sower soweth the word. And these are they by the way side, where the word is sown; but when they have heard, Satan cometh immediately, and taketh away the word that was

> sown in their hearts. And these are they likewise which are sown on stony ground; who, when they have heard the word, immediately receive it with gladness; And have no root in themselves, and so endure but for a time: afterward, when affliction or persecution ariseth for the word's sake, immediately they are offended. And these are they which are sown among thorns; such as hear the word, And the cares of this world, and the deceitfulness of riches, and the lusts of other things entering in, choke the word, and it becometh unfruitful. And these are they which are sown on good ground; such as hear the word, and receive it, and bring forth fruit, some thirtyfold, some sixty, and some an hundred. And he said unto them, Is a candle brought to be put under a bushel, or under a bed? and not to be set on a candlestick? For there is nothing hid, which shall not be manifested; neither was any thing kept secret, but that it should come abroad. If any man have ears to hear, let him hear. And he said unto them, Take heed what ye hear: with what measure ye mete, it shall be measured to you: and unto you that hear shall more be given. For he that hath, to him shall be given: and he that hath not, from him shall be taken even that which he hath. And he said, So is the kingdom of God, as if a man should cast seed into the ground; (Mark 4:14-26).

Jesus even told us that if we don't understand this parable, we won't understand any parable. He said this is the foundational parable for understanding any other parable in the entire Bible. It's the law of seedtime and harvest.

I want to break this passage down so we can understand it.

> Behold, a sower went forth to sow; and these are they by the wayside where the word is sown, but when they have heard, Satan cometh immediately… (Mark 4:14-15a).

In these first verses, we see that satan is a dust eater. He's the lion who goes about seeking whom he may devour (1 Peter 5:8) by taking away the Word sown in their hearts.

> And these are they likewise which are sown on stony ground; who when they have heard the word, immediately receive it with gladness, and have no root in themselves (Mark 4:16-17a).

I want us to focus on verse 18, which says, "And these are they which are sown among thorns; such as hear the word," The Bible says, "And these are they." What is "they"? "They" refers to seeds. The Word of God is a seed, and this parable of seedtime and harvest is the foundational parable of the entire Bible. It says, *"These are seeds sown among thorns."* In this statement, Jesus points to Adam's sin bringing the curse to the garden, as evidenced by the thorns and thistles. In this verse, He directly refers to sowing under the curse—sowing among thorns, which is doing God-things but doing them without the blessing. Doing the right things, but without God's favor on them.

> And the cares of this world, and the deceitfulness of riches, and the lusts of other

> things entering in, choke the word, and it becometh unfruitful (Mark 4:19).

Jesus said unfruitfulness is the result of sowing among thorns. Thorns are an indication of unfruitfulness. He was saying that when you sow among thorns, it's not going to bear fruit for you. If your life is unfruitful in results, you might be sowing among the thorns. You might be living your life in the wrong ground. You might be investing your life in the wrong thing. You might be heading in the wrong direction. You might be doing something God doesn't want to bless because if He blessed it, you might feel like it was a license. You might be doing the opposite of what He wants you to do with your life.

If you feel like you are just hitting a wall, you might be. Notice Jesus gave you three things in verses 19 that are indicators of it. The **first i**ndicator is the cares of this world or the worries of life.

**Next** is the deceitfulness of riches. Proverbs 23:4 tells us we should not labor to be rich. Does God want you rich? Yes, but He doesn't want riches to own you. If riches get in the way of you obeying God with your life, then they are in the way. We don't make decisions about our lives just because we may get rich doing it. We make decisions about our lives because it's the will of God for us. We don't take a career path so that we will get rich. We take a career path because it's what God wants us to do, and it'll be a blessing to Him and others. He will take care of the riches; you take care of doing the right thing. You do what's right; God will take care of the riches part.

**Finally**, the lust for other things indicates that your life is unfruitful. The deceitfulness of riches and the desire for other things enter your life. So, you have to put other things to the side. The primary thing is the primary thing. If a man loses his life for God's sake, he will find it. The primary thing is the will of God. Lose yourself in Him, and you will discover what life is really about.

**Lose yourself in Him, and you will discover what life is really about.**

So, here we find that thorns are an indication of an unfruitful life. You are sowing your life where it does not need to be planted.

## GET JESUS IN YOUR BOAT

Let's look at Mark 6:

> And straightway he constrained his disciples to get into the ship, and to go to the other side before unto Bethsaida, while he sent away the people. And when he had sent them away, he departed into a mountain to pray. And when even was come, the ship was in the midst of the sea, and he alone on the land (Mark 6:45-47).

Notice that the disciples are going to the other side, and Jesus goes to a place to pray. Instead of getting in the boat, Jesus leaves to pray at the mountain.

> And he saw them **toiling** in rowing; for the wind was contrary unto them: and about the fourth watch of the night he cometh unto them, walking upon the sea, and would have passed by them (Mark 6:48, emphasis added).

Jesus sees the disciples toiling in the boat. But how did He see them? It's dark, and they are in the middle of the lake. Jesus saw it in the Spirit. He didn't have a set of binoculars looking out at them; He knew it and saw them in the Spirit.

In this verse, we see the word "toiling" again. If you remember, to "toil" is to work when you are running against the grain. It's when you row the boat up the stream and have nothing to help you. One of the ways to be led by the Spirit of God is to be led by favor. If you can't find God's favor in what you're doing, you're probably doing the wrong thing. You do what you can, but you must trust Him to do what you can't do.

**One of the ways to be led by the Spirit of God is to be led by favor.**

Once again, these disciples are trying to row the boat up the stream against the wind. When I read this, I'm reminded of the old song lyrics, *"You don't tug on Superman's cape. You don't spit into the wind. You don't pull the mask off that old Lone Ranger…"* ("You Don't Mess Around with Jim," 1972). You just don't do what's not blessed.

I want you to notice the terminology in Mark 6:48. Here are the disciples in a thorn patch, in a boat going nowhere. They are rowing with no movement. It's like cutting wood using a dull axe with no chips flying. They are working without anything happening—much work without any benefit.

Jesus saw their toil and left His place of prayer to help them. He walked on water to reach them in the middle of their situation. And notice what it says, "…and [He] would have passed by them" (Mark 6:48c, emphasis added). If you want God's help, you better ask Him to get in your boat with you because He will walk right by you in the middle of the storm and let you row in conflict with the wind. Just because you believe He can do something doesn't mean He will do anything. He would have walked right by His disciples in the boat.

But they summoned Him:

> But when they saw him walking upon the sea, they supposed it had been a spirit, and cried out. For they all saw him, and were troubled. And immediately he talked with them, and saith unto them, Be of good cheer: it is I; be not afraid. And he went up unto them into the ship; and the wind ceased: (Mark 6:49-51a).

When Jesus got into the boat, the wind ceased. The ground is cursed by sin, and life on this planet is cursed in every capacity by the taint and struggle of sin. Unless Jesus gets into your boat, you will just have to live with it. You are going to live by your wits; you are going to live by your own prowess and abilities. I would rather live with God in my boat. I would rather live with Jesus living in my house. I'd rather have His blessing than any amount of work I could do on my own.

> And he went up unto them into the ship; and the wind ceased: and they were sore amazed in themselves beyond measure, and wondered (Mark 6:51).

Jesus is now in the boat with the disciples. When Jesus gets in the boat, all the contrariness in life suddenly diminishes. That doesn't mean everything in life will work great for you, nor will everything be a beautiful bed of roses. I'm not saying that. Many times, we struggle for much too long over things we should have given up long ago. We can't seem to find God's favor on it, regardless of how hard we look. We spend our lives trying to do things that don't have a blessing. Life's significantly too short to go anywhere without Jesus.

As the old southern gospel song goes, "I won't walk without Jesus. I won't talk without Jesus. I refuse to live one day without the Lord." I want Him in my boat. I want Him in my corner. Dead-end job, dead-end life—dead-end everything brings no satisfaction. You can't sleep at night for the torment. You can't pay the bills; you're upside down all the time. Enough already! When Jesus gets into your boat, everything is better.

We are talking about supernatural provision—not natural provision. If natural methods worked, we would just work hard to make it. However, I'm talking about the **supernatural** element that goes beyond natural ways and means. You hear about the Ways and Means Committee in Congress, but the Holy Ghost is our Ways and Means Committee. He will show us the way and provide the means.

God will show us the way and provide the means.

Let's go to the book of Luke:

> Now when he had left speaking, he said unto Simon, Launch out into the deep, and let down your nets for a draught. And Simon answering said unto him, Master, we have **toiled** all the night, and have taken nothing: nevertheless at

> thy word I will let down the net. And when they had this done, they enclosed a great multitude of fishes: and their net brake. And they beckoned unto their partners, which were in the other ship, that they should come and help them. And they came, and filled both the ships, so that they began to sink (Luke 5:4-7, emphasis added).

Toil doesn't produce. Working with the blessing is what produces. The disciples toiled with the fish all night but caught nothing. However, as soon as Jesus got involved, unfruitfulness was over. That which wouldn't produce now suddenly produces like crazy! The land without the blessing brings about nothing, but the land with the blessing blossoms like a rose.

With the blessing of God on them, these disciples caught so many fish that two boats almost sank with the weight, and they knew where to sell those fish, too. They knew how to turn them into cash. That's supernatural provision. The hand of the Lord becomes involved in what you do, doing for you what you can't do for yourself.

Look at the children of Israel when they returned to Israel. History tells you that the Promised Land was so barren that it could hardly sustain life. However, after the children of Israel returned to the Promised Land after being exiled in Egypt, it began to blossom. That land was under a curse for the other people because it was not their land. When the rightful owner came back, the ground began to produce. It's still producing. More patents come out of Israel than any other country in the world.

# 10
# More to Redemption

Many things happened at Calvary. There is a whole series of events that we think about in relation to Calvary, but this redemptive story is not just Jesus on the cross; there is much more to it. There was a resurrection; without that, the trip to the cross would have been in vain. Many have hung on a cross, but only one defeated death, hell, and the grave. So, without the resurrection, the trip to the cross would have meant nothing. Without the resurrection, the babe in a manger would have meant nothing. Plenty of babies were born in Jesus' time, but only one went to the cross and was raised from the dead. He changed everything.

## THE COMPLETE PICTURE

As these stories unfold, we don't always see the complete picture of what God is doing. However, as we look back, we see things more clearly. Let's look at the book of John:

> Now there was leaning on Jesus' bosom one of his disciples, whom Jesus loved. Simon Peter therefore beckoned to him, that he should ask who it should be of whom he spake. He then lying on Jesus' breast saith unto him, Lord, who is it? Jesus answered, He it is, to whom I shall

> give a sop, when I have dipped it. And when he had dipped the sop, he gave it to Judas Iscariot, the son of Simon. And after the sop Satan entered into him. Then said Jesus unto him, That thou doest, do quickly (John 13:23-27).

Jesus shared a meal with Judas, His betrayer. From there, Jesus went to Gethsemane, and His sweat became great drops of blood, which was a redemptive act in and of itself. Without the shedding of blood, there is no remission of sin. His blood began to be shed before He arrived at Calvary. There was a process of redemption working through Him.

One of the processes of redemption is found in Matthew:

> Then the soldiers of the governor took Jesus into the common hall, and gathered unto him the whole band of soldiers. And they stripped him, and put on him a scarlet robe. And when they had platted a crown of thorns, they put it upon his head, and a reed in his right hand: and they bowed the knee before him, and mocked him, saying, Hail, King of the Jews! (Matthew 27:27-29).

There's a reason this crown was made of thorns. Thorns and thistles began to spring up as a result of the curse. When sin entered, the ground was cursed, and the thorns were representative of the curse. Unfruitful labor was part of the curse.

When Jesus was on His way to Calvary's hill to hang on that hideous cross, they put a crown of thorns on His head. Those thorns were not just an accident. They were a divine impartation of an event to bring His redemptive plan to humanity.

As Jesus was crowned with thorns, the curse of the ground was placed on Him. It was the curse we couldn't get rid of—the curse we couldn't break—that He was taking for us. Jesus became a curse so we could be redeemed. The Bible says He who hangs on a cross is cursed (Galatians 3:13). Jesus was put on that cross for the curse—our curse, our sin, and the result of our sin. The sin that brought condemnation onto this planet was all carried away by Jesus. He didn't take away merely a piece of it or only a part of it; He carried it all.

Jesus is saying to us, once and for all, that the curse of the ground that keeps you from an unfulfilled life and from bearing the fruit you were put here to produce was placed on Him. Jesus took away the thing that wants to cause you to run contrary to the wind constantly, with a lack of peace and without finding your direction. It was removed with absolute certainty when they crowned Jesus with the crown of thorns. To forgive our sin alone did not require the crown of thorns on His head. We can see that there was much more taking place at Calvary.

In the process of His crucifixion, Jesus took the ground that would no longer produce and made it viable again. He made a difference between those who are under the covenant and those who are not. When you are under the covenant, the ground will produce for you. He was saying, *"I will do for you that which you can't do for yourself. I'll bring to pass for you what no one else can do. I will cause the ground to begin to produce on your behalf."* Therefore, the days of cursed living should be over for every child of God.

However, if you don't know what Jesus did, He will walk by the boat and won't get in there with you. You won't have access to what you need. He wants to be in your boat. Are you going to let Him in it? He wants to do for you what you can't do yourself. He wants to connect you to answers. He wants to put the wind at your back in your favor—not contrary to what you need. He wants to do things that you can't even imagine.

> And when they had platted a crown of thorns, they put it upon his head, and a reed in his right hand: and they bowed the knee before him, and **mocked him**, saying, Hail, King of the Jews! (Matthew 27:29, emphasis added).

Jesus took away our humiliation. The redemptive plan allowed Jesus to put answers in our hands for the cursed ground under which we live. After His resurrection, we see it illustrated in His life with Peter, who felt guilt and shame for his betrayal of the Lord. In the book of John, we read of Peter's guilt:

> Simon Peter saith unto them, I go a fishing. They say unto him, We also go with thee. They went forth, and entered into a ship immediately; and that night they caught nothing (John 21:3).

When reading that verse, it would be easy to assume Peter was just going out for a day on the lake since he was a fisherman. However, that's not what he was saying; He was saying:

> *I'm going back to fishing. I'm leaving the ministry. I betrayed the Lord, and I'm not worthy to do this anymore. I feel the guilt, shame, and stain of everything I've done. I'm not worthy to carry this*

> *gospel. I'm going to go back to being a fisherman because I know how to do that. I'm leaving this fruitful and favored life and going back to do it my way.*

When you start doing things by the arm of the flesh, what used to produce for you will not necessarily produce for you anymore. You can't rely on your wits and human skills like you used to do it. Before coming to God, you were one thing. Now that you've been to God, you're another person, and you must remember that. Once you put your hand to the plow, do not look back. Things won't produce for you the same way they did in the past. **You are not here to live a memory; you are here to live a future.**

> But when the morning was now come, Jesus stood on the shore: but the disciples knew not that it was Jesus. Then Jesus saith unto them, Children, have ye any meat? They answered him, No. And he said unto them, Cast the net on the right side of the ship, and ye shall find. They cast therefore, and now they were not able to draw it for the multitude of fishes (John 21:4-6).

The disciples caught no fish on their own. When Jesus gets involved in your circumstances, there is a multitude of fish in your future. You can toil all night and take nothing, or you can do it His way and find the purpose for living. You can do it His way and gain an abundant life. Jesus said, "I have come so that they may have life and have it in abundance" (John 10:10b, HCSB).

# RICH IN GOD

Blessing is the absence of thorns, thistles, and the curse. In Proverbs, we see what the blessing of the Lord. Again, the Bible says:

> "The blessing of the Lord, it maketh rich, and he addeth no sorrow with it" (Proverbs 10:22).

This verse did not say you get rich through your wits, human effort, and hard work. God teaches hard work, but He says hard work is not enough. We must have the blessing of the Lord. The blessing is what makes you rich.

You may say, *"I don't want to be rich."* Well, okay, but the blessing also makes you prosperous in what you do. It is what gives you fulfillment in what you do. The blessing of the Lord makes us rich, but not just financially. If you are financially wealthy and totally dissatisfied with life, you're not rich; you just have a lot of money. There's a big difference between being satisfied and dissatisfied. Many people with a lot of money are not rich because they are not rich unto God.

In Deuteronomy, it says:

> But thou shalt remember the Lord thy God: for it is he that giveth thee power to get wealth, that he may establish his covenant which he sware unto thy fathers, as it is this day (Deuteronomy 8:18).

This verse tells us not to forget the Lord. You must remember Him. Don't forget that it's God who gives you the power to get wealth!

There is a power to get wealth, and it's more than just hard work. You must work, but there's another power at work here. Is hard work enough? No. **Supernatural provision is the blessing that allows us to enjoy life and see the fulfillment of what we were put on this earth to do.** I'm not talking about a lot of money. Some people give up money to be in the will of God because they would rather be in God's will than have steamer trunks full of cash. I would give up money to be in God's plan because the will of God is not for sale. God wants you to be rich in Him, not just wealthy with stuff.

You often hear the phrase, *"I just work for a living."* It's good to work and labor with your hands. Ephesians 4:28 says:

> Let him that stole steal no more: but rather let him labour, working with his hands the thing which is good, **that he may have to give to him that needeth** (Ephesians 4:28, emphasis added).

The Scripture says you don't work for a living. It says you work for the seed you need to establish your future. Your prosperity is not based on your work; your prosperity is based on God's grace and His gift to you. So, you don't work for a living but to have seed to sow for your future. Your income is not contingent on what you make; your income is based on what you sow. You work for the seed that will give you your future.

Someone might think, *"Well, I'm on a fixed income."* The only thing that needs to be fixed about you is your heart, which is fixed, trusting in the Lord (Psalm 112:7). That's the only thing that needs to be fixed. We don't live on fixed incomes. You unfix any income by sowing it. You don't have to sow it all, but it's wise to keep some of it going out to others on a regular basis.

When you work to have seed to sow, it changes your whole concept about everything. You might say, *"The only way He can prosper me is through my check."* I believe God is bigger than that, and we have a promise! The Bible tells us, "Knowing that whatsoever good thing any man doeth, the same shall he receive of the Lord, whether he be bond or free" (Ephesians 6:8). You can be retired or not retired, bond or free. It doesn't make any difference to God. Any condition, level, or status doesn't matter; this will work for you.

If you want your life to take on a new dimension, make something good happen for someone else. What you make happen for others, God will see to it that it happens for you. This promise should eliminate all jealousy. You help someone get to the top, and God will see to it that you get there, too. We're talking about *Jehovah Jireh*. The way to supernatural provision is not up; it's down. If you don't want to rule, be a servant.

**What you make happen for someone else, God will see to it that it happens for you!**

The Bible says:

> Cast thy bread upon the waters: for thou shalt find it after many days... In the morning sow thy seed, and in the evening withhold not thine hand: for thou knowest not whether shall prosper (Ecclesiastes 11:1, 6a).

What you put in the ground will return to you because the ground is no longer cursed for you. That ground will produce!

# 11

## Remember Where It Came From

Imagine several people gathered in a room in random positions, all looking at an object in the center. Each person sees it from a unique point of view. One person sees it from one angle and another from a different angle. When we share everyone's perspective, we see the object differently than we did at first. In the same way, you can look at a Bible story from different points of view and see aspects of it that you possibly never knew existed.

Let's dissect a passage in 1 Corinthians:

> Moreover, brethren, I would not that ye should be ignorant, how that all our fathers were under the cloud, and all passed through the sea; (1 Corinthians 10:1).

This verse references the children of Israel being led by God with a cloud by day and a pillar of fire by night. God used this way to provide direction and protection to them in the wilderness. The cloud spared them from Pharaoh's army that was coming to destroy them; it blocked the army. That cloud was for direction and guidance, but it was also something that protected or surrounded them from their enemies. The Bible also says they passed through the sea, talking about when they crossed the Red Sea.

Let's continue in 1 Corinthians 10:

> And were all baptized unto Moses in the cloud and in the sea; And did all eat the same spiritual meat; And did all drink the same spiritual drink: for they drank of that spiritual Rock that followed them: and that **Rock** was Christ. But with many of them God was not well pleased: for they were overthrown in the wilderness (1 Corinthians 10:2-5, emphasis added).

Notice that the word "Rock" is capitalized, which is a reference to Christ. So, this is a type of Jesus. This passage says God was not pleased with Israel's overthrow. He gives us a clear illustration of that here. *Overthrow* can refer to a lot of things. You can be overthrown by sin. Things in life can overthrow you, overpower you, or keep you from your destination. God does not want you to be overthrown; it does not please Him. So, the Lord is pleased if you complete what He intends for you to complete, finish God-given tasks, and fulfill your life's purpose or destiny.

## DON'T FOLLOW THEIR EXAMPLES

Reading on in this passage:

> Now these things were our examples, **to the intent** we should not lust after evil things, as they also lusted. Neither be ye idolaters, as were some of them; as it is written, The people sat

> down to eat and drink, and rose up to play. Neither let us commit fornication, as some of them committed, and fell in one day three and twenty thousand. Neither let us tempt Christ, as some of them also tempted, and were destroyed of serpents. Neither murmur ye, as some of them also murmured, and were destroyed of the destroyer. Now all these things happened unto them for **ensamples**: and they are written for our admonition, upon whom the ends of the world are come, Wherefore let him that thinketh he standeth take heed lest he fall (1 Corinthians 10:6-12, emphasis added).

These stories were told as examples for us. Why would God want to give us an example? To prevent the thing that happened to them from happening to us. His intent or intention was so that we would not fall into the same traps and problems that overthrew them. So, these things are our examples to prevent us from being overthrown.

Each event mentioned in this passage of Scripture references a story that took place in the wilderness; you can go back and read them all. One such story mentioned was when the idolaters built a golden calf to worship. A lot of events were capsulized in this passage as the apostle Paul admonishes us to take spiritual inventory of our lives so we don't fall into these things. We don't want to think everything's good when maybe it's not. So, we should all regularly take spiritual inventories of our lives.

There are five things mentioned in this passage from 1 Corinthians that contributed to Israel's overthrow. As we pass through here, it's good to look and see what's there.

**1. Lust for evil things.**

Lust is not necessarily sexual. Obviously, it can be, but lust is the desire for something that God says you can't have. If you want something God says you can't have, that's lust. It's a desire to have or to do what God has placed off limits. It's when you want something that is outside what's permissible. The children of Israel wanted something God said they couldn't have. They desired something God said was off limits.

**2. Idolatry.**

The second thing is idolatry, which takes on many forms. The people Moses was leading built a golden calf, which was clearly an idol, but we sometimes have more sophisticated idols. For instance, yours may be a bass boat or a custom Jeep® you want to take off-road. Time to meddle: It could be your kid's soccer practice or your son's Little League™ baseball team. When you start putting those things above the house of the Lord and your service to God, they have become idols to you. We can do this with anything.

You might say, *"Well, we've got to do these things."* No, you **MUST** bring your children up in the nurture and admonition of the Lord. When these other things take precedence over what's mandated, they become idols to you. I'm not saying these activities are wrong—it's not improper to do these things. These things are not sinful unless you give them a priority to which they are not entitled.

Someone could say, *"I'm not going to build a golden calf."* Sometimes, it's more duplicitous than that. Things have ways of intruding into our lives, and we don't pick up on them quickly enough. Idolatry is out there waiting.

**3. Fornication.**

Obviously, "fornication" can have a sexual connotation. But, if you'll notice, this passage says twenty-three thousand were destroyed because of fornication. It appears that it was not over sexual sin but rather over rebellion against God. Their error was fornication against the spiritual laws of the kingdom of God. They were lusting after something other than God, and He called that fornication. As we read our Bibles, we must be careful because we can have one way of looking at a word, but the Hebrew and Greek words are usually much more broad than that.

**4. Tempting Christ.**

Tempting Christ was another thing that caused their failure. What is it to tempt Christ? If we look at Ananias and Sapphira, we see that lying to the Holy Spirit is tempting Christ. The Bible says not to make a vow to God unless you intend to keep it because if you fail to keep it, you are tempting Christ. Lying to the Holy Spirit and making promises you don't keep to God are two ways to tempt Christ.

Another way to tempt Christ is by failing to discern the Lord's body. When you come into a relationship with God, you enter into a covenant with Him, which means you enter into a covenant with His body. The Bible says you must treat those covenants properly, or else many are weak, sick, and prematurely die because they did not discern the Lord's body (1 Corinthians 11:29). This principle extends further than just communion. When you join a church, one may say, *"I didn't sign a covenant or a contract."* Yes, you did when you agreed to become part of the church, agreeing to support it, be part of it, and make it better. The body of Christ is universal in nature, but it's also talking about the local body you attend. When God speaks to you about being part of the church, He's talking about the one you attend. Ignorance about these things is never an excuse.

**5. Murmuring and complaining.**

Another thing that allows us to be overthrown is murmuring. The word "murmur" means to complain. The children of Israel had the joy of stretching out a two-week trip into a 40-year expedition because they murmured against God.

If you want to live in your trouble, grumble about it because that is the opposite of praise. The Bible says that we are to praise our way out of trouble. If you gripe while in trouble, you will stay in it. To complain or murmur is to declare that God is incapable of helping us. To murmur is saying things like, *"He wouldn't get me out of my situation or move on my behalf."* Murmuring is a lack of faith in God. We are to praise our way out of trouble!

## MANNA FROM HEAVEN

Again, these things were written as examples for us. There's a story unfolding in Exodus chapter 16:

> Then said the Lord unto Moses, Behold, I will rain bread from heaven for you; and the people shall go out and gather a certain rate every day, that I may prove them, whether they will walk in my law, or no (Exodus 16:4).

Here, we find God raining bread from heaven. Remember, our topic is supernatural provision. It doesn't take much revelation to see this is not the norm. God rained bread from heaven for you. In other words, this verse is saying that you can get a certain amount of manna each day. You can gather enough for you but not enough to give everyone a multi-day supply; otherwise, it would rot. You are to remember the Sabbath and keep it holy by not gathering any bread on that day, so you must collect enough the day before to see you through. When you pick up a two-day supply before the Sabbath, the bread will not rot. However, you can't gather more any other day, or it will rot. So, that's supernatural in and of itself.

*Manna* is a type of the Word of God. In your spiritual walk with the Lord, you need to gather some spiritual food daily. God is saying you can't stock up on revelation from God. You can't get enough today to last you a year. You can't put it in your backpack. You must feed on it every single day. You must get something from God every day. So, manna is a type or model of hearing from the Lord. Man shall not live by bread alone but by every word that proceeds out of the mouth of God (Matthew 4:4). So, manna is a type alluding to every word God speaks.

Later in this chapter, we find these instructions regarding the manna:

> And in the morning, then ye shall see the glory of the Lord; for that he heareth your murmurings against the Lord: and what are we, that ye murmur against us? (Exodus 16:7).

According to Exodus, God had been feeding the children of Israel with quail; they tired of it and started complaining. So, God gave them manna to replace the quail. They started murmuring against the manna, so they got more quail. They had so much quail that they didn't want anymore.

We have ways of griping and complaining about God's provision. Sometimes, it becomes so common to us that we no longer see His hand. We can be so familiar with the blessing of God that we no longer see it as anything special or supernatural. These people began to murmur against God concerning His provision. If God quit providing food for them, they would die because they are in the wilderness with no Piggly Wiggly®.

Now, let's go on a little further in this same chapter:

> And when the dew that lay was gone up, behold, upon the face of the wilderness there lay a small round thing, as small as the hoar frost on the ground. And when the children of Israel saw it, they said one to another, It is manna: for they wist not what it was. And Moses said unto them, This is the bread which the Lord hath given you to eat (Exodus 16:14-15).

This word "manna" means *"What is it? What is this?"* They called it "manna" because they had never seen it before. To my knowledge, it has never been seen again. Manna was there for a season of time. They couldn't do much with it, but it sustained them for forty years. God fed them with manna for forty years, and they didn't even know what it was.

The book of Mark talks about sowing seeds without understanding how they grow:

> And he said, So is the kingdom of God, as if a man should cast seed into the ground; And should sleep, and rise night and day, and the

> seed should spring and grow up, he knoweth not how (Mark 4:26-27).

*The children of Israel were probably asking, "What is it? How's He going to get this to me?"* You don't have to know how; you just need to know Him. You don't have to understand where He's going to get it. You don't have to know if it's behind door number one, two, or three, but you can rest assured God will come by it honestly. He won't have to steal it. He will get it to you the right way. God has ways of meeting our needs in very supernatural ways.

## A RIGHT ATTITUDE

Now, I want to focus our attention on Deuteronomy 8. I don't think there's anywhere in the Bible that is more descriptive of God's provision than this chapter. There may be other chapters equal to this one, but I don't think any are better at describing what God wants to do for those who are His. This chapter also issues some instructions related to God's provision. We are talking specifically in this chapter about from where the provisions come. These verses tie back to those things we covered in 1 Corinthians chapter 10 and Exodus chapter 16. Let's take a look:

> And thou shalt remember all the way which the Lord thy God led thee these forty years in the wilderness, to humble thee, and to prove thee, to know what was in thine heart, whether thou wouldest keep his commandments, or no (Deuteronomy 8:2).

In other words, God is saying that some of these things will become tests because God may withhold some things from us. Understand, however, that God doesn't withhold things from us because He doesn't want us to have them. God withholds things because He wants you to have the right attitude about them. For instance, have you ever seen a spoiled child? Why would you withhold things from them? It's not because you want them to go without; it's because you want them to have a better attitude about things. Next verse:

> And he humbled thee, and suffered thee to hunger, and fed thee with manna, which thou knewest not, neither did thy fathers know; that he might make thee know that man doth not live by bread only, but by every word that proceedeth out of the mouth of the Lord doth man live (Deuteronomy 8:3).

So, God humbled Israel by feeding them manna. That verse tells you that manna is a type of the Word of God that comes down from heaven. Man does not live by natural bread alone but by every word that proceeds from His mouth, and He compares it to manna. Continuing on to the next verse:

> "Thy raiment waxed not old upon thee, neither did thy foot swell, these forty years" (Deuteronomy 8:4).

Their clothes didn't wear out, and their feet didn't swell. This would be a good verse to confess if you stand up all day on a concrete floor. You see the hand of the Lord in this supernatural provision. Let's go to verse nine:

> A land wherein thou shalt eat bread without scarceness, thou shalt not lack any thing in it; a land whose stones are iron, and out of whose hills thou mayest dig brass. When thou hast eaten and art full, then thou shalt bless the Lord thy God for the good land which he hath given thee (Deuteronomy 8:9-10).

God's desire is for you to experience surplus, not scarcity. He is not withholding your provision. He might be altering attitudes, but He is not short on provisions.

## THE CONDITION

Do you think the children of Israel had a better covenant than we do? The Bible says that Jesus bought and paid for a better covenant with better promises. So, if we have a lesser covenant with lesser promises, Jesus went to Calvary in vain. However, that's not the case. The Old Covenant was insufficient, and it took a "trip" to Calvary to finalize that. Therefore, they didn't have a better covenant than you and I. They didn't have more provisions than we have. If anything, Israel had less than what we have. In this passage, we find them eating their bread without scarceness, lacking nothing.

This passage shows that God is giving Israel a land without scarceness, withholding nothing from them. However, this life without scarcity hinges upon the following verse:

> **Beware** that thou forget not the Lord thy God, in not keeping his commandments, and his judgments, and his statutes, which I command thee this day: (Deuteronomy 8:11, emphasis added).

God is saying, *"I want to bless you; I want to give you a life without scarceness. My desire is to give you whatever you need. I want to give you every possible thing you will ever need—all things that pertain to life and godliness."* However, there's a condition. God said, "Beware!" Why does He use the word "beware"? The word *beware* is there as a warning. Be warned. Be careful. Watch how you think about this.

We can live in the land of abundance and forget about God. There's a tendency to remember the Lord during the lean years, but when we come into the fullness of that which we believed God, we forget about Him. We start having things we only dreamed about and take it all for granted. Somehow, we get the idea that our hard work or extraordinary abilities got us here.

You might have great abilities and incredible giftings, but all it takes is one heart attack, and you don't have it anymore. Just one little thing happens, and you lose it. That's when things can hit close to home. I'm not saying that God does these things, but it can happen, and our attitudes can quickly become humble. It's essential to keep a right attitude.

If you open the door to the devil, you get what the devil gives. I want to offer perspective on how quickly things you take for granted can be lost. You are just one breath away from losing it. One phone call or one event can change your world. **However, if your faith and trust are in God, then an event cannot change the fact that God is still your provider.** Phone calls happen to everyone, but when you know God is your supernatural provider, you don't have to be blown out of the water. You don't have to be devastated.

## A STORY OF PROVISION

My dad was 93 when he passed away; he lived a long, healthy life. But, when you get older, you get to where you can't do some of the things you used to do. Dad really wanted to stay in his house, but it got to the point where he couldn't. We tried to make ways for him to stay as long as he could, but finally, something had to be done. The kind of care he needed was expensive. Out of the blue, Dad received a nice inheritance from a source we couldn't imagine. What 90-year-old gets an inheritance from anyone? For the next few years, he didn't pay one penny out-of-pocket for his care; that inheritance covered it all. I'm talking about supernatural provision from the God who provides. *Jehovah Jireh* knew what my dad would need and how to get it to him from a source you could never predict in a million years. I saw it happen, and I was in awe. As his caretaker, God provided for me, too.

When you are in the midst of situations, you don't always see things as clearly as when you look back on them. I was amazed watching this happen with my dad. If there's ever an illustration of the supernatural provision of an Almighty God, this is absolutely it. Beware, lest you forget who's behind it. We knew exactly who was behind this blessing because we know the God of the Bible.

It may start as an unexpected phone call, and you don't know what it all means until you work your way through the process. The next thing you know, it's the hand of provision. God has ways of providing for you. It may be a phone call you didn't expect. It may be a letter in the mail you didn't know was coming. There could be some set of events or chance meetings. Someone could write you into their will. You don't know how God is going to supply for you, but He will.

We must know in whom we have believed. You may not know how God is going to do it, but we go to bed, and we get up. The seed springs up and grows; we don't know how (Mark 4:26-29). That's a perfect illustration of it. It's just the hand of the Lord.

## REMEMBER GOD

Let's read from Deuteronomy 8 again:

> Beware that thou forget not the Lord thy God, in not keeping his commandments, and his judgments, and his statutes, which I command thee this day: Lest when thou hast eaten and art full, and hast built goodly houses, and dwelt therein; And when thy herds and thy flocks multiply, and thy silver and thy gold is multiplied, and all that thou hast is multiplied; (Deuteronomy 8:11-13).

God doesn't want you living in a closet–sized house unless that's what you want. He wants you to live in a goodly house—not build a goodly house and then have to sell it because you can't afford it. He doesn't want you to be like the people who work on an assembly line and build new cars they can never drive. God's best is for us to *build goodly houses and dwell therein.* His best is for our herds and flocks to multiply! I have a beagle at home, and I would have ten beagles if Nora, my wife, would let me. We would have fun at my house! The Bible says you can build a goodly house and live in it while your herds and your flocks multiply along with your silver and gold.

Some people say, *"I don't believe God wants me to prosper."* Well, I'll take your part. The Bible says your silver, gold, and all you have is multiplied. The provision of Almighty God is not scarceness and lack; God's provision is abundance.

The next verse reads:

> Then **thine heart be lifted up**, and thou forget the Lord thy God, which brought thee forth out of the land of Egypt, from the house of bondage (Deuteronomy 8:14, emphasis added).

When your heart gets lifted up, that's an indication of pride. You start to think, *"I did that."* You believe it was your skill or luck that accomplished something. When living an abundant life, we tend to forget that the hand of the Lord brought it to us. The Bible tells us not to forget where it came from; we must remember God. God's caution comes because it's easy for us to forget.

Continuing in this passage of Scripture, God said:

> "And thou say in thine heart, My power and the might of mine hand hath gotten me this wealth" (Deuteronomy 8:17).

In other words, *"I did it by my own mechanisms—my own devices—my own savvy. I'm smarter than others. I took the short-cut routes, and I outmaneuvered them."* No, the hand of the Lord gave it to you.

## THE BLESSING

The next verse is significant. It says:

> But thou shalt remember the Lord thy God: for it is he that giveth thee power to get wealth, that he may establish his covenant which he sware unto thy fathers, as it is this day (Deuteronomy 8:18).

There's a caution in this passage when it talks about God's provision. When you dwell in goodly houses, and all your possessions multiply, God said to be careful not to think that you did it. The caution is to "remember the Lord thy God: for it is he that giveth thee power to **get** wealth" (Deuteronomy 8:18, emphasis added). An important word is used here. According to the Hebrew scholar Gesenius, the word "get," as in "get wealth," means to procure, gather, bring forth, manufacture, produce, or create. **God has given us the power to create wealth.**

If you listen to various movements, they believe the earth has a limited amount of resources. They don't think wealth is produced by God; instead, it's created by man. These groups believe that wealth exists and there's only so much to go around. They say, *"You mean old billionaires; the poor have nothing because you have so much."* There may be some truth to that in some places where people have misused and mishandled their positions. However, taking from the rich to give to the poor is what the Bible calls coveting another man's wealth, and that's prohibited in the Ten Commandments. That's as basic as you get. It doesn't matter how much someone else has; you're not entitled to it if it's not yours.

Over-taxing the rich to give to the poor does not work. That situation will make both the poor and the rich poverty-stricken so that politicians can have it all. If you think socialism works, you know nothing about the Scripture.

A zero-sum world believes there is one pie; if we slice it up enough, everyone gets some. However, the one-pie theory doesn't work. Do you remember the little boy's lunch in the Bible? The little boy took his lunch to Jesus. When He blessed and broke it, the boy's lunch became enough to feed a multitude. God has given you the ability to create more than what is here, which becomes wealth creation. God has put in your hands the power to create wealth. We are never at the point of "this is all there is." It may have been all there is until you got there, but the blessing of the Lord makes more. There's no better illustration of this than feeding the multitude with a little boy's lunch twice—with a few loaves and some fish. A boy took it to the hillside, and once the blessing hit it, his little became a multitude. God has the power to take your little bit and breathe life into it where little becomes much.

If we look at Moses' story, he started making excuses why he couldn't do what God was calling him to do. Then God asked him, *"What's in your hand?"* He answered, *"I have a stick."* God *said, "That's all I need. Just bring your stick. I don't need much. Give me anything to work with."* Little becomes much when the hand of God is on it. The blessing of the Lord, it maketh rich, and He adds no sorrow with it (Proverbs 10:22).

When the blessing of God gets on the pie we were talking about, it's not just a pie anymore. Ask that little boy. He brought his lunch to Jesus, and a multitude was fed with it. When they cleaned up after everyone finished eating, 12 baskets of leftovers went home with the little boy. He gave his lunch to Jesus and got 12 baskets in return, plus fed a multitude. When God blesses something, it will bless the recipients and the giver. That little boy didn't go home broke; he went home with more than lunch. He went home with the hand of God on his life.

From these verses, we see that the blessing of the Lord makes you rich. Now again, remember it's the Lord thy God who gives you the power to get or create wealth. Here's this verse in the Amplified:

> But you shall remember [with profound respect] the Lord your God, for it is He who is giving you power to make wealth (Deuteronomy 8:18a, AMP).

When you put your hand on something, a supernatural power comes into it that makes wealth. Something that did not exist now exists because you put your hand on it. It did not exist before, but it comes into existence when your hand is on it. The blessing of the Lord, **it** makes you rich.

Let's revisit Proverbs 10:

"The blessing of the Lord, it maketh rich, and he addeth no sorrow with it" (Proverbs 10:22).

Earlier, we talked about "toil." We see that word here in another translation:

"The blessing of the Lord—it makes [truly] rich, and He adds no sorrow with it [neither does toiling increase it]" (Proverbs 10:22, AMPC).

Hard work is essential, but it is not hard work alone that causes you to prosper. The Bible says that if you don't work, you don't eat (2 Thessalonians 3:10); you need to work. However, it's not hard work that brings the blessing. In fact, the only result of hard work alone is that you get tired. Hard work **without the blessing and favor of God on it** is just hard work.

Let's look at this verse in the New International Version:

"The blessing of the Lord brings wealth, without painful toil for it" (Proverbs 10:22, NIV).

I like the way it reads in the Good News translation:

"It is the Lord's blessing that makes you wealthy. Hard work can make you no richer" (Proverbs 10:22, GNT).

It's not your hard work, prowess, competence, or mental abilities that prosper you. It's not because you are so savvy that you know how to do it better than anybody. It's the blessing of the hand of God on your life that will sustain you, feed you, enlarge your herds and flocks, increase your wealth, and multiply your gold and silver. It's the blessing of Almighty God.

Once it starts flowing, you must remember who brought it to you. Never take it for granted or believe you got it just because you are sharp. You may be smart, but you need more than that. Scripture does say God makes you wiser than your teachers (Psalm 119:99), so I'm not putting that down. However, you can have degrees from the most prominent universities on the planet, and without the blessing of the Lord, it will not prosper you. It is the blessing of the Lord that makes rich.

I want us to look at Nehemiah:

> And refused to obey, **neither were mindful of thy wonders that thou didst among them**... Thou gavest also thy good spirit to instruct them, and withheldest not thy manna from their mouth, and gavest them water for their thirst. Yea, forty years didst thou sustain them in the wilderness, so that they lacked nothing (Nehemiah 9:17, 20-21, emphasis added).

This passage says the children of Israel forgot from where their blessing came and were not mindful of His wonders. So, we must be mindful; we cannot forget what God has done. Israel forgot that God gave them their blessings.

Proverbs 23 says:

> Wilt thou set thine eyes upon that which is not? for riches certainly make themselves wings; they fly away as an eagle toward heaven (Proverbs 23:5).

I want to emphasize that it's the blessing of the Lord that makes rich, but if we forget Him, the blessing has ways of disintegrating.

## GOD'S BENEFIT PACKAGE

The Bible tells us, "Blessed be the Lord, who daily loadeth us with benefits..." (Psalm 68:19). God's benefits are not just money. His benefits include health for your body, peace of mind, unspeakable joy, a fulfilled life, a family with friends, and more. Psalm 103 tells us not to forget all His benefits:

> Bless the Lord, O my soul, and forget not all his benefits: Who forgiveth all thine iniquities; who healeth all thy diseases; Who redeemeth thy life from destruction; who crowneth thee with lovingkindness and tender mercies; Who satisfieth thy mouth with good things; so that thy youth is renewed like the eagle's (Psalm 103:2-5).

God has a benefit package for you. When you remember God and give Him praise and worship, He will allow you to keep it. You will build goodly houses and dwell in them. You will not have to sell your goodly homes because you can't pay for them. God will bless you and let you keep your benefits if you remember from where they came.

Your riches will not make themselves wings and fly away. That's for someone else who does not remember Him. That does not apply to me. I choose to remember the Lord my God, who gives me the power to get wealth.

If my wealth runs out, I'll put my hand on something else because the blessing comes with me when I get there. We don't have to go somewhere to be blessed; we take the blessing with us. It's blessed when you get there because you bring God on the scene. Your presence becomes the breakthrough because God gives you the power to create and acquire wealth.

You must work, but you can't work enough to offset the curse. You can't work that hard. You can't do enough. There is always something out there trying to steal from you, but it's the blessing that makes you rich without sorrow. It takes God working in you to access supernatural provision.

# 12
# The Blessing Makes You Rich

In some church circles, you are not supposed to use the word "rich" because they believe all preachers are just after your money. Sometimes, people belittle the kingdom of God in such a way that robs them of receiving from Him. Think about how many billboards you pass daily—they all want your money. However, God doesn't want your money; He wants **you** because Scripture says where a man's treasure is, there is his heart. God wants your heart, but He knows He doesn't get you without your money. So, you can't say you love God and not give Him your financial wherewithal because you spend your money on what you love.

The term "rich" is a scriptural word. It doesn't just come from something we thought up; it comes from the Bible. It says in Genesis, "Now the Lord had said unto Abram, Get thee out of thy country, and from thy kindred, and from thy father's house, unto a land that I will show thee:" (Genesis 12:1). A lot could be said about God leading Abraham, but the point is he couldn't get to his place from where he was. Abraham had to go somewhere else; he had to obey God. He was required to make a change—he had to move. Often, the things you are around get in your way. God told Abraham to leave his family and relatives.

Why is it necessary to get away from your kindred? At times, it's unnecessary, but sometimes, our family traditions can hold us back and keep us from the Word of God. Jesus said your traditions can make the Word of God of no effect. In His hometown of Nazareth, He could not do any mighty works. Note that He was capable of doing the miraculous, just not in His hometown. Why? Familiarity. All the things that went on around Him hindered Him. Let's look at Mark 6:

> Jesus left that part of the country and returned with his disciples to Nazareth, his hometown. The next Sabbath he began teaching in the synagogue, and many who heard him were amazed. They asked, "Where did he get all this wisdom and the power to perform such miracles?" Then they scoffed, "He's just a carpenter, the son of Mary and the brother of James, Joseph, Judas, and Simon. And his sisters live right here among us." They were deeply offended and refused to believe in him. Then Jesus told them, "A prophet is honored everywhere except in his own hometown and among his relatives and his own family." And because of their unbelief, he couldn't do any miracles among them except to place his hands on a few sick people and heal them. And he was amazed at their unbelief (Mark 6:1-6, NLT).

The people in this verse asked, *"Are these not His brothers and sisters around us here?"* In other words, *"We knew Jesus as He was growing up. Where does He get these things?"* Because of this attitude, they could not receive from Him. You might say they were bothered by His success and authority. The Bible says Jesus spoke as one with authority (Matthew 7:29). These people were probably disturbed by the simple fact that He didn't mince words or apologize for the truth. That's why Jesus had to leave His kinfolk.

A prophet is without honor in his hometown because they will not let him get "past his past." The people negated God's benefits because of their own ignorance. They didn't recognize the anointing, the change, and the difference in Jesus. These are essential principles that must be understood. To illustrate this, look at kids who grow up in a church. They begin to grow up, get an education, and alter their behavior. At some point, you must quit looking at them as just kids. God begins to use their lives. Our children are becoming men and women of God; they are no longer kids. They are our brothers and sisters, and we must recognize them as such.

## CONDITIONAL PROMISES

The Bible says in Genesis 12:

> Now the Lord had said unto Abram, Get thee out of thy country, and from thy kindred, and from thy father's house, unto a land that I will show thee: And I will make of thee a great nation, and I will bless thee, and make thy name great; and thou shalt be a blessing: And I will bless them that bless thee, and curse him that curseth thee: and in thee shall all families of the earth be blessed (Genesis 12:1-3).

That's when God visited Abraham to talk about the covenant He was making with him. The word "testament"—New Testament, Old Testament—means covenant. Our Bible is a copy of the covenant God made. As you read it, you are reading our contract with God.

In this passage, God's one caveat was that Abraham had to obey Him. God will do what He said **if** you do what He asks you to do. It's a conditional covenant. Every promise in the Bible, whether it states it directly or not, is understood to be conditional. There is a prerequisite that goes with it that says, *"If you do this, then I will do that."* You must know the "if" is there. The book of Isaiah says, "If ye be **willing and obedient**, ye shall eat the good of the land:" (Isaiah 1:19, emphasis added). If you are willing and obedient, you will eat the good of the land. It doesn't say you're going to eat the good of the land when you're unwilling and disobedient. So, the condition is there.

On occasion, God has someone prophesy over an individual. Then, we are quick to blame the prophet and label them a "false prophet" if it does not come to pass. We believe that they gave a false prophecy because something did not happen. You must understand that prophecies are conditional. Every prophecy has a condition on it, whether stated or not, before it will come to pass. Those prophetic words led to God's will in someone's life. It may have been God's intention, but it's not automatic that it will come to pass. People can walk out of God's will through disobedience at any time. We don't need to rush to call someone a false prophet but pray for the one disobeying God.

Years ago, I witnessed a legitimate prophet prophesy to a man with a past in front of a large crowd. The prophet gave him an outstanding word. However, the man with a history returned to the world. When none of the prophecy came to pass, people began to call the preacher a false prophet. No, the prophet stated God's will. If the man had stayed on track, that's what would happen for him. But since he didn't, it's not coming to pass. God states His will, but it is not automatic.

## ABRAHAM'S BENEFITS

Returning to our story, God made a covenant with Abraham, saying, "I will bless you." That blessing contained certain things. Look in Genesis 13:

> And Abram [or Abraham] was very rich in cattle, in silver, and in gold... And Lot also, which went with Abram, had flocks, and herds, and tents (Genesis 13:2, 5, emphasis added).

It says Abram was very rich in material things. We read about the blessing in chapter 12, and then in chapter 13, we see that cattle, silver, gold, and all those things were part of that blessing. The result of that blessing took him into a place of wealth. Abram's nephew, Lot, was under his blessing by association. You hang around with wise men, and you'll be wise. Continuing on:

> And the land was not able to bear them, that they might dwell together: for their substance was great, so that they could not dwell together (Genesis 13:6).

In other words, they had so much livestock between them that there wasn't enough grass to feed them all, so they had to split up. They didn't separate out of strife; they split up because of their great substance and no way to contain it all. That's a pretty good problem to have. I want you to see that the blessing God placed on Abraham brought great wealth and substance into his life.

Someone said, *"When you serve the Lord, you might go broke."* You might go broke because you're ignorant about your covenant. We are all ignorant about some things, but you don't need to be uneducated about God's covenant.

The Bible tells us, "And also that nation, whom they shall serve, will I judge: and afterward shall they come out with great substance" (Genesis 15:14). This verse refers to the children of Israel and their time in Egyptian bondage. God was saying, *"When they leave, I'll bring them out with great substance."* So, substance was a part of their deliverance when God brought them out. "Substance" means *stuff*. They had supernatural provision of material goods.

Look at another verse in Genesis 15:

> In the same day the Lord made a covenant with Abram, saying, Unto thy seed have I given this land, from the river of Egypt unto the great river, the river Euphrates: (Genesis 15:18).

God made a covenant with Abram [Abraham], which included substance: cattle, herds, flocks, silver, gold, and stuff. They had great substance as part of God's covenant with Abraham.

Over the ages, villainous groups have been demonically inspired against the Jewish race, and one reason is because of God's blessing on them. They are a people of covenant. The Jewish race also gave us our Savior and the Bible. All those things are offensive to the devil, so, he inflames anti-Semitism. The covenant God had with Israel is everlasting, even to this day. According to that covenant with Abraham, God blessed them with substance.

## THE PROMISED LAND

Again, we find Proverbs 10 saying, "The blessing of the Lord, it maketh rich, and he addeth no sorrow with it" (Proverbs 10:22). We talked about the word "sorrow," meaning to toil. If you read it from the Good News translation, it says it this way:

> "It is the Lord's blessing that makes you wealthy.
> Hard work can make you no richer"
> (Proverbs 10:22, GNT).

So, it is the blessing that brings wealth. We saw this when God put the blessing on Abraham. It's not **A** blessing, but **THE** blessing—**the** blessing of the Lord makes rich. Again, the Bible says if you don't work, you don't eat; you are supposed to work. However, hard work cannot make you richer. Remember, your supply is supernatural.

Hard work is natural, not supernatural. You can work hard without the blessing and just get a lot of blisters and sweat as a reward. It takes the blessing to increase. You should work hard, but working hard without the blessing is in vain.

The blessing originated with Adam, but he blew it off. God told him to subdue the world, and everything would be under his dominion. That's a big blessing. Then, God told Noah the same thing after that flood—blessing, replenish, and multiply. Now, we find this blessing given to Abraham.

Deuteronomy 8 talks about the children of Israel coming out of bondage with great substance. It says, "A land wherein thou shalt eat bread without scarceness" (Deuteronomy 8:9a). God is talking about the land He was promising them. The rest of that verse says, "Thou shalt not lack any thing in it..." (Deuteronomy 8:9b). So, God intends for there to be no scarceness in your life. Scarceness is an indication of lack.

Christians often talk and sing about the Promised Land. We talk about "going up yonder" and "crossing the chilly Jordan;" once we enter the life to come, we will enter our Promised Land. Have you ever thought about the fact that there are no giants "over yonder," but there are giants in the Promised Land? So, for the child of God in the New Covenant, the Promised Land is not "over yonder;" our Promised Land is in the here and now. The Bible says the Promised Land for you is the place of God's provision, the place of God's blessing, the place of God's substance. Our Promised Land is a land with no scarcity and no lack.

**The Promised Land for you is the place of God's provision, the place of God's blessing, and the place of God's substance.**

Some may say, *"Well, that's not possible. Our Promised Land is in heaven."* God's provision won't be the Promised Land for those who don't believe it because faith is the conduit or passageway by which you extract these things. If you don't put faith in it, it will not happen for you. But don't get mad at someone who does believe it and lives in God's provision. In the land that He promised, God said they would eat their bread without scarceness and lack for nothing. In other words, God will bring to them things that are under the earth (i.e., iron and brass) and all the things in it.

Let's look on down in that passage:

"Lest when thou hast eaten and art full, and hast built goodly houses and dwelt therein;" (Deuteronomy 8:12).

This verse says you can build a good house and live in it. It does not say you can build a good home and have it foreclosed on you. The word "mortgage" is a companion to *mortuary, mortality, and mortal.* Mortgage actually means death grip. God wants you to live in a house without a mortgage. However, most of us can't purchase a home without a mortgage, but God intends to get you out of that debt.

Some find themselves saying, *"Well, I don't see how that could ever happen for me."* It's difficult for some to imagine, but **we must project our faith to where we want to go, not where we are now.** Start believing God for it. If you don't know it's God's will, then you'll never project yourself out there for it. God said we can build goodly houses and dwell in them.

Someone could be saying, *"I know that God wants to bless me spiritually, but maybe not so much materially. He doesn't want me blessed."* That is not what He said. God promises that our goods will multiply: herds, flocks, silver, and gold. Then, He said all you have will be multiplied. So, you can see **God is not limited to spiritual blessings only.** He promised these things and warned us: Don't forget the Lord. God summed up His promise:

> But thou shalt remember the Lord thy God: for it is he that giveth thee power to get wealth, that he may establish his covenant which he sware unto thy fathers, as it is this day (Deuteronomy 8:18).

# WORKING THE PROCESS

God has given us the power to get wealth. As we defined earlier, "get" means to procure, gather, bring forth, manufacture, produce, or create. That's an interesting word. God has given us the power to create wealth. In other words, wealth would not exist unless I got involved with it or unless the covenant somehow got involved with it. It is **the blessing** that makes rich. So, it's the blessing on you that creates the outcome. It produces for you when it doesn't produce for someone else who does not have the blessing. The blessing causes wealth to come into being where there was no wealth, which proves beyond question that this provision is supernatural.

In other words, wealth materializes because you are involved with it. It only appears if you are in the equation. It shows up because you show up. So, wealth creation is part of the blessing of God. There is wealth creation and provision where there once was none.

I don't know how that happens, but the Scripture says it's a Kingdom principle. You put your seed in the ground, and you go to bed and get up. The seed springs and grows up, but you don't know how. Mark chapter four says it this way:

> And he said, So is the kingdom of God, as if a man should cast seed into the ground; And should sleep, and rise night and day, and the seed should spring and grow up, he knoweth not how. For the earth bringeth forth fruit of herself; first the blade, then the ear, after that the full corn in the ear. But when the fruit is

> brought forth, immediately he putteth in the sickle, because the harvest is come (Mark 4:26-29).

This passage does not say that you must know the minutiae of how it will all happen. You just need to understand how to work it. I don't know how it gets here; it just gets here. Isn't that what *manna* means, *"What is it?"* I don't know how it got here; it's just here. It came from heaven. It didn't exist for anyone else—only those with the blessing. The blessing of the Lord, **it** makes rich, and He adds no sorrow with it. No amount of hard work will replace God's blessing. No amount of toil—no amount of strife—no amount of struggle—no amount of human effort—can ever do more than the blessing can do. It is the blessing that makes rich, period.

God's prosperity is a supernatural provision. It is beyond the natural ways and means. It may not happen for one, but it still will happen for you **IF** you understand it. As we said earlier, when studying Mark 4, the amount of thought and attention you give these things will determine how it comes back to you. If a man sows little, he will reap little; if he sows much, he will reap much.

The amount of thought and attention you give will determine your harvest. You can't receive from God what you don't understand. If you can't articulate it, you probably can't have it. This truth is yours if you want it.

## POWER IN THE BLESSING

Do you remember the multitude that Jesus fed through God's supernatural provision? There were 5,000 men plus women and children, totaling around 15,000 people. Matthew, Mark, and

Luke all give this same story, but we will use Luke's illustration of this principle because it enables our point to be a little more concise.

> And when the day began to wear away, then came the twelve, and said unto him, Send the multitude away, that they may go into the towns and country round about, and lodge, and get victuals: for we are here in a desert place. But he said unto them, Give ye them to eat. And they said, We have no more but five loaves and two fishes; except we should go and buy meat for all this people (Luke 9:12-13).

They are in the wilderness with no Piggly Wiggly® or Food City®. It sounds a bit like the manna in the wilderness. They are in a desert place—with only five loaves and two fish. Naturally speaking, that's not nearly enough food to feed some 15,000 people. Have you ever lived in the "world of not enough"? When you live in the "world of not enough," you need a visit from the realm that has more than enough—where the supernatural is imposed over the natural. When there is not enough, we must have help to get enough.

God didn't put anything in the Bible just for fun. Everything is in there for a reason: instruction, illustration, etc. I don't believe the words in Scripture are misplaced, either. They are precise and succinct, and they mean what they say.

> For they were about five thousand men. And he said to his disciples, Make them sit down by fifties in a company. And they did so, and made them all sit down. Then he took the five loaves

> and the two fishes, and looking up to heaven, he blessed them, and brake, and gave to the disciples to set before the multitude. And they did eat, and were all filled: and there was taken up of fragments that remained to them twelve baskets (Luke 9:14-17).

Jesus fed 5,000 men, plus women and children, in this gathering. Wouldn't you agree that feeding them the way He did would be called supernatural provision? Jesus organized what they would do and how to group them. I believe God noted twelve baskets left over to emphasize that the little boy's tuna fish lunch couldn't feed 5,000 men plus their families. The leftovers were that little boy's harvest from the investment of his lunch. You can see that when you give to God, He brings back abundance into your life.

There are points in this story that are important. If you'll notice, Jesus had a little boy's lunch that, when blessed, fed a multitude. Blessed refers to the blessing of God that enabled the children of Israel to eat their bread with no lack or scarcity. It was the same blessing passed on to Abraham and Lot, which caused them to enjoy abundance. The children of Israel lived in that abundance, and Jesus knew all about the blessing. In cooperation with that blessing, Jesus released supernatural provision on the boy's tuna sandwich to feed 15,000 people. Someone who understood the process created a supply to feed the crowd that day. The blessing gave Jesus the power to create wealth.

Before Jesus blessed the food, He told His disciples, "You give them something to eat" (Luke 9:13a, NIV). Jesus told the disciples to feed the crowd before there was enough food. He was telling them, *"If you understood what I understand about the blessing, you could feed this group."* They had in their hands the power to create, also.

I believe God breathed into our lives the power to create from something that doesn't exist—the ability to multiply where it doesn't exist—the power to bring to pass things that do not exist until your hand gets put on them. Something wasn't there, but now it is.

A person could say, *"Well, I don't know where it comes from."* I don't know either, but I do know that God put in my hands the power to create wealth. Is that not precisely what Jesus did right there? But notice, it didn't happen till He spoke the blessing over it.

*"You mean there's power in the blessing?"* That's exactly what I mean. The ability to bless is the power to create wealth where it did not exist. The blessing can change things where there is impotence—where there is inability—where there is lack. There was not enough until Jesus' hands touched it.

Jesus told His disciples to feed the crowd because He knew they had the blessing, too. Jesus did nothing except by the power and anointing of the Spirit of God. He did not do it as the Son of God. My translation of John 5:19 is Jesus saying, *"I don't do anything except I see the Father do it."* In other words, He didn't do it just because He thought it would be a nice thing to feed that crowd. No, He got it from Father God. It was a download from heaven that came to Him. Jesus confirmed, "The Father that dwelleth in me, he doeth the works" (John 14:10c). The Father also dwells in you, and He does the work by the power of the Holy Spirit. When you get a download from heaven, you can lay your hands on anything, and it will multiply. That's called walking in the will of God. Without the blessing, things are barren. With the blessing, things produce.

It's not hard work alone that will get you to this place. No amount of hard work is going to do this. It requires the power of the blessing to make you rich. The blessing will make you rich. God said it's the blessing of the Lord that maketh rich.

When Jesus told His disciples to feed the multitude, it was undoubtedly something they could do if they knew how, but they had to have the download from heaven. They couldn't do it just because they wanted to do it. The disciples were capable of getting a heavenly download, or Jesus would not have instructed them to hand out food.

Look in Galatians 3, where it says:

> And the scripture, foreseeing that God would justify the heathen through faith, preached before the gospel unto Abraham, saying, In thee shall all nations be blessed (Galatians 3:8).

We began our study with Abraham. This verse says God the Father preached the gospel to Abraham, saying "in thee shall all nations be blessed." This event occurred back before Calvary, referencing Genesis 12. In other words, the gospel was the revelation of imparting the blessing. When you preach a gospel that does not contain the blessing, you are not preaching **the** gospel. You are preaching only half the gospel. The gospel God preached had wrapped in it the promise that the blessing of Almighty God will come on your life if you receive it.

If you don't tell people the complete gospel, you are not telling them the truth God wanted you to tell them. When God the Father preached the gospel to Abraham, He said, *"I'm telling you what I'm going to do for you and anyone else: If you will embrace it, believe it, and receive it, the blessing of Almighty God will start working in your life."* It is the blessing that makes you rich, and it adds no sorrow with it. The blessing of Almighty God has come on us!

## THE ROLE OF FAITH

I want to take this a little further. Let's look later in the same chapter where it says:

> Christ hath redeemed us from the curse of the law, being made a curse for us: for it is written, Cursed is every one that hangeth on a tree: **That the blessing of Abraham might come on the Gentiles through Jesus Christ; that we might receive the promise of the Spirit** through faith (Galatians 3:13-14, emphasis added).

You can't say it any clearer than what that verse says. Everything the Spirit promised, we receive through faith. You can transfer anything God says you can have to yourself by using your faith.

One thing He said is that you are a joint heir with Christ Jesus (Romans 8:17). That's yours! If you are in Christ Jesus, the blessing of God is on you—not the blessing of the Republicans, Democrats, Lima Bean Growers of America, or the United States Government. Those groups have many limitations. The government is in debt, but God's not. The blessing of Almighty

God comes on you through Christ Jesus. It is the blessing that brings about supernatural provision.

Jesus was on the hillside and took a little boy's lunch. He blessed it and multiplied it. When He put His hand on what the boy had—the hand that creates wealth—the blessing came on it, too. When the blessing came on it, miracles followed. The little boy's lunch fed the five thousand.

We've had lean times in our church. At one time, we actually put the church's checkbook in a room, playing the Word of God to it day and night, speaking life to it. We didn't go broke, but we could have. Speak the blessing over your business' books. You may need to take your bank accounts and speak blessings over them. Stand on the Word, and tell your accounts to prosper. Sanctify it for the work of the Kingdom. Set it apart for God. If your account tells you nothing is in it, command it to be fruitful and multiply. Speak the blessing of Almighty God over it! Someone may say, *"You can't do that."* You can if you believe it. You have to get to where you believe God's promises.

Look further in this chapter, and you'll see that the blessing of Abraham has come on us through Christ Jesus. It says, "And if ye be Christ's, then are ye Abraham's seed, and heirs according to the promise" (Galatians 3:29).

Everything God said to Abraham is yours—the blessing of the Lord, it maketh rich—rich in herds and flocks and silver and gold—all his substance was blessed. We haven't deviated from the topic; we are still discussing supernatural provision. We are talking about provision where there was nothing. Jesus was out in the desert with nothing but a little boy's lunch. When He put the blessing on it, there was more than enough for all.

In your hands is the power to create. Some people reading this book are waiting on God to do something, but He wants you to put your hand on something so it will multiply. Your hands have the power to create wealth. Look at your hands and say, *"These are blessed hands. They have the power to create wealth by the blessing of Almighty God."*

When you begin to believe the Bible, things start to shift. Things begin to change. When I married my wife, we were kids. We have not lived in abundance for all of our marriage, but we've never been in lack because we tithed regularly from day one. We didn't know much but knew we were supposed to tithe. Then, we learned some things about sowing seeds on purpose. Our lives have increased from that day forward. The blessing is not predicated on abilities alone, but your abilities, mixed with the blessing of God, are more than enough.

Ephesians 1:3 says, "Blessed be the God and Father of our Lord Jesus Christ, who hath blessed us with all spiritual blessings in heavenly places in Christ." This verse refers to the past tense blessing of God on you. When you put your hands on something, expect God to bless it.

The blessing of God contains three main things: forgiveness of sin, healing for your body, and a promise to provide for you. We are not alone in this world. You are not on your own; God has given you all things pertaining to life and godliness. There is supernatural provision promised for you.

# 13

# GOD ALWAYS PROVIDES

In this chapter, we will discuss how God always provides for us. Let's look at 2 Kings to see three stories that bring perspective to God's willingness to meet our needs. This is more far-reaching than the area of finance, but it includes that. If you don't have health, you can't earn money. You can't make money if you don't have a sharp mind. The woman with the issue of blood spent all she had and only grew worse; her lack of health stole her finances.

I mainly use the King James translation because of its clarity, but I use the other translations to help understand the depth of the Greek or Hebrew. The point is to understand the Word of God more clearly and use whichever translation it takes.

## HEALING THE WATER

2 Kings 2:19 from the King James Version says, "And the men of the city said unto Elisha, Behold, I pray thee, the situation of this city is pleasant, as my lord seeth: but the water is naught, and the ground barren."

The Amplified Classic makes this verse more clear:

> And the men of the city said to Elisha, Behold, inhabiting of this city is pleasant, as my lord sees, but the water is bad and the locality causes miscarriage and barrenness [in all animals] (2 Kings 2:19, AMPC).

That difference is why I often read from the Amplified Classic translation; there are things here that you can't see in the King James. This verse says the water in Jericho causes miscarriages and barrenness in the animals. You can imagine that the same things could also happen to people. The water is toxic and causes health issues. The city that it's talking about here is Jericho, whose water supply was contaminated or poisonous. Let's look further at the prophet Elisha in 2 Kings:

> He said, Bring me a new bowl and put salt [the symbol of God's purifying power] in it. And they brought it to him. Then Elisha went to the spring of the waters and cast the salt in it and said, Thus says the Lord: **I [not the salt] have healed these waters; there shall not be any more death, miscarriage or barrenness [and bereavement] because of it**. So the waters were healed to this day, as Elisha had said (2 Kings 2:20-22, AMPC, emphasis added).

The water of Jericho was not just healed for the moment. It underwent an eternal cleansing of the water supply for the people. Whatever the source of the problem, God supernaturally did something about it through the instructions to the prophet and his willingness to act on the Word of God. God led the prophet to put salt in it to restore and heal the water forever. Before there was refrigeration, people cured meat with salt to preserve it for later use. Salt was so important that people sometimes paid with it. However, it was scarce, and many did not have access to it. In those places, it was analogous to gold. The importance of salt is because it's a life-giver. Salt is a type or archetype of a purifier or preservative.

In the Christian's case, we are the salt of the earth—a societal purifier. We are to take the light and life of God to a world that's in trouble and needy. So, we become the salt of this world. Salt has many different ramifications; it's a type in many ways. It also represents covenant; there is a covenant of salt. God was working in the people of that region by using salt to represent a covenant blessing on those people.

We are talking about supernatural provision. These people were losing their livestock and children were dying early because of the water. God saw it and was concerned about it enough that He intervened by doing some things to change their situation. *Jehovah Jireh*—the God who is more than enough—God, the Provider—saw their predicament. He saw their dilemma and said, *"I'm going to create some circumstances that will change this for you, not just today, but I'm going to change this for you forever. I'm going to move supernaturally on the prophet whose job it is to manifest my will in the earth, and he's going to do certain things that will cause you to walk in the blessing from the present and on into the future. I'm going to change your circumstances beyond the natural"* Again, notice what it says:

> Then Elisha went to the spring of the waters and cast the salt in it and said, Thus says the Lord: I [not the salt] have healed these waters; there shall not be any more death, miscarriage or barrenness [and bereavement] because of it (2 Kings 2:21, AMPC).

This verse shows salt as a representative or type. "Salt" is a word we should look into and think about because God was saying something by using it. He could just as easily have put dirt, sand, or rocks in it. God could have said anything He wanted because He is the one who did it. However, He didn't say to use those other things; He said to put salt in it.

Some believe that healing is in the salt. That same logic has been used about the parting of the Red Sea. You hear of some people trying to downplay the parting of the Red Sea by saying it was only three inches deep where Moses and the people crossed. I don't know which is the bigger miracle: parting the sea or drowning Pharaoh's army in three inches of water! You can look at it any way you want to look at it, but God had to do something. On a miracle scale of one to ten, both would tie for a ten!

I don't know which is the bigger miracle: parting the sea or drowning Pharaoh's army in three inches of water!

Someone always has an explanation. However, you missed the point if you think the salt healed the water. That's why I wanted you to see this verse in another translation. In the Amplified Classic, the Lord said He healed the water. Salt becomes representative of covenant, a type of the Christian life. It represents wages or His blessing. You probably heard the idiom, "He is not worth his own salt." That saying refers to wages. Salt represents a lot of things. So, this was a supernatural event. God, our supernatural Provider, healed the waters and gave the people a good place to live. I've been to Jericho, and it is a nice place. However, "nice" is a relative term; I would rather be in Honolulu.

The children of Israel were saying that inhabiting this city is pleasant, but there are some problems with the water supply. So, God, the supernatural Provider, blessed the water. The blessing of the Lord, it makes rich. God changed the economy when you consider losing livestock. It was an economic miracle, too. God, the supernatural Provider, moved on their behalf.

The Scripture says these things are given as examples. When brought into the light of the New Testament, God gives us these things to illustrate His hand on us. God cares about you. He doesn't leave you out of anything. The Lord is as engaged in your life as you are; He's closer to you than your breath. There's not a thing you think, ask, want, desire, cry about, or long for that He doesn't know about and is not concerned about. God is not off somewhere far away; He's involved and engaged in your life.

## HEALING THE POT

There is another story with Elisha as the protagonist or chief character in 2 Kings chapter four. The setting for this story is the protracted events involving the sons of the prophets from the school of the prophets and the Shunammite woman. Now, Elisha returns to Gilgal, where Scripture says:

> And Elisha came again to Gilgal: and there was a dearth in the land and the sons of the prophets were sitting before him: and he said unto his servant, Set on the great pot, and seethe pottage for the sons of the prophets (2 Kings 4:38).

In other words, they are making a meal. Remember, there is a famine in the land, so there is a shortage of food and supplies.

Now, seminary students don't know much. How do I know? I used to be one. It takes a while to know things. You can see the youthful enthusiasm, but a lack of knowledge manifested in this verse:

> And one went out into the field to gather herbs, and found a wild vine, and gathered thereof wild gourds his lap full, and came and shred them into the pot of pottage: for they knew them not (2 Kings 4:39).

This seminary student was going to gather herbs but instead found a wild vine. It wasn't a grapevine; it was a wild vine with gourds. In that part of the world, it was probably a species of cucumber. It's speculative because the Bible doesn't tell us exactly what it was. These students didn't know what they were doing. One gathered food because of the famine and decided to cook whatever he found.

> So they poured out for the men to eat. And it came to pass, as they were eating of the pottage, that they cried out, and said, O thou man of God, there is death in the pot. And they could not eat thereof (2 Kings 4:40).

I told you that they didn't know what they were doing. There's death in the pot. Now, that's a bad meal. I've been to some restaurants and thought, *"This is not the best chicken I've ever had."* However, I have never had the thought that it would kill me! It might be a little tough—might not be as tasty as I'd like—but I don't think it will kill me. I don't know what caused them to say that there is death in the pot. Maybe they were suddenly and violently ill. But whatever the case may be, they quit eating it. It was more than just tasting bad; they had a reaction to it. The bottom line is they couldn't eat it. Look how Elisha responds:

> But he said, Then bring meal. And he cast it into the pot; and he said, Pour out for the people, that they may eat. And there was no harm in the pot (2 Kings 4:41).

Elisha uses the meal here just like he used the salt earlier. What does meal or flour have to do with death in the pot? Nothing. Again, the meal represented the hand of God's blessing, the supernatural provision of Almighty God. When there's a famine in the land, Elisha has them bring some meal, and he puts it in the pot. Meal, in and of itself, does not have the ability to do away with poison. Eating sufficient quantities of the stew could have proved deadly. A supernatural event occurred because the stew could now be eaten.

The point here is we find a similar story of adding salt to the bitter water. Now you find a gourd with death in it, and God somehow intervenes to prevent that death cycle from taking place in the people. The supernatural hand of an Almighty God made it so that there was not only enough for them to eat, but other people also ate from it.

In the middle of a famine—with not enough food to eat—God showed them how to feed the people with a supernatural hand. Different events, certainly, but it sounds a little like the loaves and fishes that we covered earlier. There, we saw multitudes in the wilderness with insufficient food, and God told His disciples to give them something to eat, but they didn't know how to respond.

If there is famine in the land, it really doesn't matter how much money you have. If there is no food, you can't buy any. You can have all the money you need but still can't buy it. In addition to the food, there are financial ramifications. If you have sufficient money, you could go and buy it. But in this case, money wouldn't do them any good. In a way, these are the same as financial miracles. The reason I'm making this point is because sometimes people divorce one thing from another when reading the Bible. They see God do a water miracle or a food miracle, and they don't equate that to having financial ramifications. They fail to see the economic crossover.

However, if you go to the grocery store today and step up to the register, they request payment for your food. For the most part, getting food requires money. If you have money, you get it; if you don't have money, you don't. The Bible says *if you don't work, you don't eat,* which connects money to food. Here again, God emphasizes His provision and ability to provide when there is no natural ability to provide it.

## FOUR LEPERS

There is a similar story in 2 Kings, chapters 6 and 7:

> And it came to pass after this, that Benhadad king of Syria gathered all his host, and went up, and besieged Samaria. And there was a great famine in Samaria: and, behold, they besieged it, until an ass's head was sold for fourscore pieces of silver, and the fourth part of a cab of dove's dung for five pieces of silver (2 Kings 6:24-25).

The armies of Syria are besieging the area of Samaria. They are under attack, and there is a famine and lack in the land. Again, this perfectly illustrates why I like to compare translations. Let's read verse 25 in the Amplified Classic:

> And a great famine came to Samaria. They besieged it until a donkey's head was sold for eighty shekels of silver, and a fourth of a kab of dove's dung [a wild vegetable] for five shekels of silver (2 Kings 6:25, AMPC).

I don't want to be too graphic, but I do want to illustrate this. If you've spent much time in the Orient—and I have spent a lot of time there—you know that the main staple of their diet is rice. One way they flavor rice is to put fish heads in with it and cook it. Now you can imagine why a donkey's head might be worth some money in a famine. We can also see from the Amplified Classic that dove's dung is a vegetable.

Let's follow this story by going to 2 Kings 7:

> Then Elisha said, Hear ye the word of the LORD; Thus saith the LORD, To morrow about this time shall a measure of fine flour be sold for a shekel, and two measures of barley for a shekel, in the gate of Samaria (2 Kings 7:1).

This passage speaks of a severe famine. The prophet put his reputation on the line and says tomorrow—not next week, next month, next year, or the next harvest—a measure of flour will sell for a shekel and two measures of barley for a shekel. Now, that's a prophetic word! It took courage to say that, and you better know God is speaking when you say something so specific or date sensitive.

> Then the captain on whose hand the king leaned answered the man of God and said, If the Lord should make windows in heaven, could this thing be? But Elisha said, You shall see it with your own eyes, but you shall not eat of it (2 Kings 7: 2, AMPC).

Elisha responded by telling the captain, *"DON'T QUESTION! You'll see it; you just won't get to enjoy it because you questioned."* Remember, we are to believe God's prophets, and we will prosper (2 Chronicles 20:20).

Someone may say, *"Well, it doesn't make any sense."* The word of the Lord doesn't always make sense; the word of the Lord makes faith, and faith comes by hearing the Word. This story continues:

> Now four men who were lepers were at the entrance of the city's gate; and they said to one another, Why do we sit here until we die? (2 Kings 7: 3, AMPC).

Here are four leprous men crying out, *"Why sit we here till we die?"* Sometimes, you may find yourself in a predicament where you will produce the same results if you keep doing what you're doing. On occasion, you have to change your location, direction, or activity. That's the end result of where these lepers arrived. They were saying, *"Hey guys, we're dying right here. We might as well do something else because staying here is not going to do it for us."* Sometimes in life, that's where we end up. Have you ever been in a dead-end job? The fearful may say, *"We might starve if we change."* You're starving now. What's the difference? You might as well starve in motion.

> If we say, We will enter into the city, then the famine is in the city, and we shall die there: and if we sit still here, we die also. Now therefore come, and let us fall unto the host of the Syrians: if they save us alive, we shall live; and if they kill us, we shall but die (2 Kings 7:4).

These lepers were saying, "*Maybe they'll have mercy on us and take us as prisoners of war and feed us, but we're going to die here anyway.*" You can see the predicament. They decide to move forward. The next verse says:

> And **they rose up** in the twilight, to go unto the camp of the Syrians: and when they were come to the uttermost part of the camp of Syria, behold, there was no man there (2 Kings 7:5, emphasis added).

Sometimes you just need to rise up! They went to the Syrian army's camp, and nobody was there. No one was camped there; the enemy was gone. Read on:

> For the Lord had made the host of the Syrians to hear a noise of chariots, and a noise of horses, even the noise of a great host: and they said one to another, Lo, the king of Israel hath hired against us the kings of the Hittites, and the kings of the Egyptians, to come upon us (2 Kings 7:6).

These four lepers, who could barely walk, went to the enemy's camp, and God somehow amplified the sound they made to sound like an army with chariots and horses in motion. In actuality, they couldn't make much noise on their own, but God made it sound like an army of chariots—a great army. He made it sound like a vast army coming to besiege them. The Syrians heard a great host, but it wasn't real. **God has ways of stopping your enemies.** He has ways of turning your captivity if you get up and believe instead of sitting there until you die.

> Wherefore they arose and fled in the twilight, and left their tents, and their horses, and their asses, even the camp as it was, and fled for their life (2 Kings 7:7).

The army left at twilight, probably in the evening. No one was coming, but the enemy ran for their lives in terror, leaving everything behind. They didn't even try to grab things as they ran away. They just left it all—their livestock, tents, and everything in the tents.

> And when these lepers came to the uttermost part of the camp, they went into one tent, and did eat and drink, and carried thence silver, and gold, and raiment, and went and hid it; and came again, and entered into another tent, and carried thence also, and went and hid it (2 Kings 7:8).

Remember, there was a famine, but they went into a tent, eating and drinking. **God has ways of feeding you in a famine.** God could set you on an iceberg in the North Atlantic, and if you call on His covenant, He will feed you. I don't know how, but He will do it. There is no situation on this planet that God cannot overcome, overwhelm, and change to your favor because you serve *Jehovah Jireh*, the God who provides—the God who is more than enough. When you don't see any way to do it, God does it anyway. That's who you serve!

You are not limited to the mechanisms of this world. If God needs it, He has a manna oven in heaven designed with your name on it. He will create circumstances and do whatever it takes. It's not too hard for Him. Do you think these are impossible circumstances that we are reading about—totally impossible? We can only say, *"But God!"* The Most High God, the Creator of heaven and earth, the God who is more than enough, is not limited. The Bible promises, "There is no restraint to the Lord to save by many or by few" (1 Samuel 14:6). He will deliver you by many or few.

**There is no situation on this planet that God cannot overcome, overwhelm, and change to your favor.**

In this passage, we see a financial miracle, too. Some people think, *"God doesn't want you to have anything. He will feed you, but He won't give you finances."* That's not what we read above in 2 Kings 7:8; it says God gave them food, drink, silver, gold, and clothes. They took their bounty and hid it. Let's go to the next verse:

> Then they said one to another, We do not well: this day is a day of good tidings, and we hold our peace: if we tarry till the morning light, some mischief will come upon us: now therefore come, that we may go and tell the king's household (2 Kings 7:9).

In other words, this verse says, *"We better tell the others because once they find out what's happening and see what we did, we'll be in trouble if we don't. We already hid our portion. They will want to know why we are down here eating and didn't tell anyone."* These lepers did the right thing after reality set in once their bellies were full and their treasure was hidden.

We are talking about the group of lepers that were going to sit there until they died. Once they decided to get up and move, they saw the hand of the Lord in action. God created circumstances that ran their enemies completely away, leaving behind many provisions. Our next verse reads:

> And they went after them unto Jordan: and, lo, all the way was full of garments and vessels, which the Syrians had cast away in their haste. And the messengers returned, and told the king (2 Kings 7:15).

This passage says that after Israel's king and army came down to the Syrian camp, they saw where their enemy had thrown things off as they left—tossed aside the things that weighed them down. Their enemy left a trail as they hurried away. Next verse:

> And the people went out, and spoiled the tents of the Syrians. So a measure of fine flour was sold for a shekel, and two measures of barley for a shekel, according to the word of the Lord (2 Kings 7:16).

What did the prophet say in verse one of this passage? Let's look at it again:

> Then Elisha said, Hear ye the word of the Lord; Thus saith the Lord, To morrow about this time shall a measure of **fine flour be sold for a shekel, and two measures of barley for a shekel,** in the gate of Samaria (2 Kings 7:1, emphasis added).

The word of the Lord told them what was coming, that one measure of flour and two measures of barley would each sell for a shekel at the enemy's gate the very next day. God became the providing God.

Verses 17 through 20 of second Kings chapter seven tell what happened to the skeptic who would not believe God could open the windows of heaven:

> And the king appointed the lord on whose hand he leaned to have the charge of the gate: and the people trode upon him in the gate, and he died, as the man of God had said, who spake when the king came down to him. And it came to pass as the man of God had spoken to the king, saying, Two measures of barley for a shekel, and a measure of fine flour for a shekel, shall be to morrow about this time in the gate of Samaria: And that lord answered the man of God, and said, Now, behold, if the Lord should make windows in heaven, might such a thing be? And he said, Behold, thou shalt see it with thine eyes, but shalt not eat thereof. And so it fell out unto him: for the people trode upon him in the gate, and he died (2 Kings 7:17-20).

The Bible says to obey His prophet so shall ye prosper (2 Chronicles 20:20). The flip side of that can have you end up with real problems. God is using this story as an example. He does not want this man to die, but you can't mock God. Ask Ananias and Sapphira what it costs to tempt God. The captain who doubted was tempting God. He cast a bad light on the word of the Lord, so he didn't get to eat of it.

## HE CARES FOR YOU

These are inspiring stories. Three spectacular events of our supernatural Provider transpire in only a few chapters. Each one has financial ramifications or financial impacts. People had a basic need and were going to die. So, God provided water and food during times of famine.

In this day and age, He could bring it in by water truck. If your water is cut off for a while, you may get an interstate pipeline with big tanker trucks bringing it in. But they didn't have any of that available to them. There was no infrastructure to bail them out. It was either get it or die with no middle ground. The supernatural hand of the providing God—the *Jehovah Jireh* God of Glory—who promised to meet your needs is the same one who did it for them. It's recorded for us, so we will know that **if He did it before, He will do it again**.

If you have a need, this is the one to whom you look. God's hand is not short; He's not slack. Regardless of where you are, God wants to provide for you. He wants to be the great Provider of your needs. He is God Almighty, who is not just enough, not barely enough, but He is the God who is more than enough, and we have a covenant with Him.

Again, when they put salt in the water, it represents a salt covenant. We have a covenant, and Abraham's blessings have come on us through Christ Jesus. Jesus was the mediator of a better covenant full of better promises. We serve a covenant-making, covenant-keeping God. When you came to Him through Christ Jesus, you entered into a covenant that says: *I, Jehovah Jireh, promise and most solemnly swear to you that I will meet your need according to my riches in glory. I will do it now, tomorrow, and eternally. You are not alone in this world. You are not on your own.*

You have a God who is not the God of barely enough, but He is the God of abundance. God Almighty wants to supply for you abundantly, not barely. I'm talking about abundant supply. If you need a job, He will get you one. If you need a raise, He will get you one. It doesn't matter what you need. He's more than enough, and He knows about you.

Let's look at the book of Mark:

> And Jesus answered and said, Verily I say unto you, There is no man that hath left house, or brethren, or sisters, or father, or mother, or wife, or children, or lands, for my sake, and the gospel's, But he shall receive an hundredfold **now in this time**, houses, and brethren, and sisters, and mothers, and children, and lands, with persecutions; and in the world to come eternal life (Mark 10:29-30, emphasis added).

What have you given up for Him? Notice, He didn't put husbands and wives on that list! Just in case someone has any wild ideas. Whatever you forsake, God has a hundredfold for you **now in this time**.

Jesus said, "Fear not, little flock; for it is your Father's good pleasure to give you the kingdom" (Luke 12:32). God takes pleasure in doing outrageously wonderful things for you. How much more shall the Heavenly Father give good things to them that ask Him? There's none good but one, and that is God. Our good God wants to come into your life in a good way and do good things for you. He is not limited; He is not without. He is the God who owns the cattle on a thousand hills, all the gold under the hills, and everything else that's in there. He owns it all, and He cares completely and totally about you.

# 14

# Miracle Debt Cancellation

In this chapter, I want to discuss miracle debt cancellation from the Word of God. This is still supernatural provision, but with a slightly different focus.

I want to qualify it going in that supernatural debt cancellation can be like believing in divine healing. We believe God is a supernatural healer and performs miracles; we don't apologize for that because the Bible is full of examples. However, our beliefs do not exempt us from the obvious things we must do in caring for our bodies as it relates to our health. For example, just because God is a supernatural healer doesn't mean we should neglect going to the doctor. I don't think that, and I would never say that. Nonetheless, I absolutely believe that God does over and above what a doctor can do, but I believe in what doctors can do, as well.

Following that same logic, the same thing holds true concerning miracle debt cancellation. Since God can miraculously cancel debt, you might say there is no responsibility on your part by thinking, *"I don't have to manage my money. I don't have to discipline myself. I can just spend and spend with reckless abandon."*

I heard a true story about this obese woman who went to her prayer group, and they cast a spirit of gluttony out of her. After that, she thought she could eat anything she wanted, and it would all be okay. I don't think that's exactly what God had in mind.

Sometimes, we hear a truth from God's Word and think it exempts us from disciplining ourselves and doing the right things, but it doesn't. Even though God is a miracle debt canceller, it does not allow us to live undisciplined to the point where we create additional debt that requires God to give us a miracle. If we begin to think that, we miss the point. Through our lack of personal discipline or self-control, we create more problems for ourselves.

## THE MESSIAH

Let's look at Luke chapter four. Jesus used this passage of Scripture to set the tone for His earthly ministry over the next three and a half years. This chapter is the earmark—guide—blueprint—for what He was put on this earth to establish. The Lord took passages from Isaiah 61 when He taught the people and proclaimed what He was called to do. It meant a lot to the people around Him. We'll explain as we go.

Luke says:

> And he came to Nazareth, where he had been brought up: and, as his custom was, he went into the synagogue on the sabbath day, and stood up for to read. And there was delivered unto him the book of the prophet Esaias. And when he had opened the book, he found the place where it was written (Luke 4:16-17).

Jesus was a churchgoer. It was His custom to go to the house of the Lord. Some may say, *"Well, I don't need to go to the brick-and-mortar church building. I have the internet today."* No, as His custom was, He went to God's house. Following His example, church attendance should be our custom, too.

Here's what Jesus read when He opened the book of Isaiah:

> The Spirit of the Lord God is upon me; because the Lord hath anointed me to preach good tidings unto the meek; he hath sent me to bind up the brokenhearted, to proclaim liberty to the captives, and the opening of the prison to them that are bound; To proclaim the acceptable year of the Lord, and the day of vengeance of our God; to comfort all that mourn; To appoint unto them that mourn in Zion, to give unto them beauty for ashes, the oil of joy for mourning, the garment of praise for the spirit of heaviness; that they might be called trees of righteousness, the planting of the Lord, that he might be glorified (Isaiah 61:1-3).

For clarity's sake, here are the same verses from the Amplified Classic:

> The Spirit of the Lord God is upon me, because the Lord has anointed and qualified me to preach the Gospel of good tidings to the meek, the poor, and afflicted; He has sent me to bind up and heal the brokenhearted, to proclaim liberty to the [physical and spiritual] captives and the opening of the prison and of the eyes to

> those who are bound, To proclaim the acceptable year of the Lord [the year of His favor] and the day of vengeance of our God, to comfort all who mourn, To grant [consolation and joy] to those who mourn in Zion—to give them an ornament (a garland or diadem) of beauty instead of ashes, the oil of joy instead of mourning, the garment [expressive] of praise instead of a heavy, burdened, and failing spirit—that they may be called oaks of righteousness [lofty, strong, and magnificent, distinguished for uprightness, justice, and right standing with God], the planting of the Lord, that He may be glorified (Isaiah 61:1-3, AMPC).

Jesus, speaking of Himself, said, *"The Spirit of the Lord is upon me because He has anointed me to preach the gospel to the poor."* Jesus found Himself in the Scripture and presented it to the gathering by quoting Isaiah's prophecy. The crowd knew this was a Messianic prophecy; they understood it was related to the coming Messiah. Reading this aloud doesn't necessarily make you the one it's talking about, but we see what Jesus did after reading. Read on in Luke 4:

> And he closed the book, and he gave it again to the minister, and sat down. And the eyes of all them that were in the synagogue were fastened on him. And he began to say unto them, **This day is this scripture fulfilled in your ears** (Luke 4:20-21, emphasis added).

That comment changed everything. Jesus wasn't just quoting Isaiah; He was saying this is happening here and now. Jesus closed the book, gave it to the minister, and sat down. It changed everything because now they wanted to stone Him.

Jesus began to tell them some important things, but in their anger and attempt to shut Him up and shut Him down, they did not let Him finish what He wanted to say. Jesus had just begun telling them; He had more to say.

## FAVOR & JUBILEE

The Lord read from Isaiah 61, saying, "The Spirit of the Lord God is upon me." Again, He refers to Himself in this passage. Preaching the gospel to the poor is part of Jesus' ministry—not just His ministry at that moment in time, but His continuing and ongoing ministry. He is called to preach the gospel to the poor, to heal the brokenhearted, and to preach deliverance to the captives. All these are part of the ministry today as we follow the Lord as head of the church. He leads us to bring recovery of sight to the blind and set at liberty those who are bruised. He's the head of the church, and we take our lead from Him. That is precisely what the church is called to do.

When you see that He's called to preach the gospel to the poor, does that mean the economically poor? It could, but it's not limited to that. The Bible says everyone separated from God is poor in spirit. So, poverty comes at a lot of different levels.

Remember, our topic is miracle debt cancellation. Do you believe in that? It's important for you to believe these things because you only get from God what you believe.

I want to focus on a particular part that Jesus proclaimed. He said that the Spirit of the Lord was on Him "to preach the acceptable year of the Lord" (Luke 4:19). When reading that statement, you can read right past it and not see what actually is going on in that verse. If we read that from the New American Standard, it says: "To proclaim the favorable year of the Lord" (Luke 4:19, NAS). It's not just the acceptable year of the Lord; it's a year when God favors certain people in some special way. It's a favorable year of the Lord. Another translation says, "To proclaim the year of the Lord's favor" (Isaiah 61:2, NIV).

Do you want the favor of God on your life? That's what Jesus was dealing with there. You have people who say, *"Well, you know, you shouldn't claim God's favor."* However, this is what Jesus came to give. If you don't lay hold of this, it's an offense to Him, as if He died in vain. If you don't receive it, none of it applies to your life.

*Someone else may say, "Well, I don't think you should believe God for favor."* If that's the case, then why did He put that in there? It's not just a space filler. Did He use words loosely by throwing that promise in there? Did it mean anything? So, hopefully, we can agree that it means proclaiming the year of the Lord's favor.

I want to share this verse from other translations so you can understand this is God's Word, not just something we came up with to tickle your ears. Now, let's look at ***The Passion Translation***:

> "I have come to share the message of **Jubilee**,
> for the time of God's great acceptance has begun" (Luke 4:19, TPT, emphasis added).

*Jubilee* is an important word, so we will look at it from ***The Expanded Bible***, which elaborates the meaning of the original language:

> "{He has sent me} to announce [proclaim] the time [year] when the Lord will show his kindness [favor; Is. 61:2; an allusion to the release of slaves during the Jubilee year; Lev. 25]" (Luke 4:19, EXB, emphasis added).

This verse alludes to the release of slaves during the Jubilee year. Here's the entire verse explaining the Jubilee from Leviticus 25:

> "Make the fiftieth year a special [consecrated; holy] year, and announce freedom [liberty] for all the people living in your country. This time will be called Jubilee [a word related to the Hebrew for "ram's horn"]. You will each go back to your own property, each to your own family and family group" (Leviticus 25:10, EXB).

Let's go back to Luke chapter four. ***The Voice Bible*** translates it this way:

> "In short, the Spirit is upon me to proclaim that now is the time; this is the jubilee season of the Eternal One's grace" (Luke 4:19, VOICE).

In the King James version, we have the acceptable year of the Lord; however, we clearly see from other translations that it refers to the Year of Jubilee. This is a biblically accurate reference. These translations are by scholars who study and dig, knowing the meanings behind these words. The margin in my King James Bible says "Jubilee," and it may say that in your Bible, too. Jesus was proclaiming the Jubilee.

Jesus went on to say, "This day is this scripture fulfilled in your ears" (Luke 4:21). He did not say the Scripture was fulfilled in the calendar cycle like under the Old Covenant. Jesus is saying that He did away with the calendar. He said, *"I am your Jubilee."* It's not in the cycle of years that brought the Jubilee; it's in a person. Your Jubilee is in Jesus.

If you want to learn more about the Jubilee, you should study it in more depth from Leviticus 25. We will not take time to read the entire chapter but will look at a few verses:

> And thou shalt number seven sabbaths of years unto thee, seven times seven years; and the space of the seven sabbaths of years shall be unto thee forty and nine years. Then shalt thou cause the trumpet of the jubile to sound on the tenth day of the seventh month, in the day of atonement shall ye make the trumpet sound throughout all your land. And ye shall hallow the fiftieth year, and proclaim liberty throughout all the land unto all the inhabitants thereof: it shall be a jubile unto you; and ye shall return every man unto his possession, and ye shall return every man unto his family (Leviticus 25:8-10).

In other words, there were seven of the seven-year cycles, which would be 49 years. At the end of the 49th year, they would sound the trumpet, and it would start the 50th year, which was the Year of Jubilee.

This passage tells them to hallow or make holy the fiftieth year and proclaim liberty. If you will remember, ***The Expanded Bible*** says the Jubilee alludes to the setting free of slaves or those who were captive. That means if a family inheritance is given, for example, a piece of land passed from generation to generation, it is to be returned to the original landholder. With this understanding, if a person were to "buy" the land, they were actually renting it. They could not purchase the land; it was a land lease and must be returned. They couldn't hold it for more than 50 years.

I was reading from a scholar discussing what the Jubilee could do. It could eliminate abject poverty because people would not be hopelessly in debt forever. There would be a time coming when there would be a new beginning. The Jubilee would also stop the accumulation of wealth at oppressive levels. It would prevent a landowner or person with tremendous resources from buying up everyone and everything because of their strength. Eventually, there would come a certain time when that activity would be dissolved. So, it stops the oppressed from being oppressed and the oppressor from oppressing.

You see the wisdom of God in doing this! It's absolutely amazing how wise God is when you see what He does with certain things. We may think about why He does something, but now we begin to see why.

> A jubilee shall that fiftieth year be unto you: ye shall not sow, neither reap that which groweth of itself in it, nor gather the grapes in it of thy vine undressed. For it is the jubilee; it shall be holy unto you: ye shall eat the increase thereof out of the field. In the year of this jubilee ye shall return every man unto his possession. And if thou sell ought unto thy neighbor, or buyest ought of thy neighbor's hand, ye shall not oppress one another: (Leviticus 25:11-14).

In the Jubilee, you can't work the ground; you have to give it a rest. In addition, everyone in the Jubilee year gets a fresh start. When the Bible was written, there was servitude, and some parts of the world had debtor's prisons. Bankruptcy laws and things of that nature forbid debtor's prisons in the United States—that's a good thing. However, in that day, there was oppression of the poor where a person could get into debt and have to go into servitude to work off their debt. Bond slaves became indebted to the person they owed for a period of time.

So, that's why Jesus said it's time to let the oppressed go free in Luke 4:18. Of course, the devil's the oppressor, and he can oppress in a thousand different ways. However, Jesus is not talking about oppression in every way; He is talking and dealing specifically with financial debt.

Some believe that God doesn't have anything to do with our finances. Biblically, that is not even close to the truth. When Jesus told us not to oppress one another, He was talking about economic oppression to the point where people are subservient to debt.

Now, I believe some people attempt to put large numbers of people under oppression through debt. Certain mechanisms, even in our government, are set in place to oppress people with debt. If you don't believe that, look at how many people currently have student loans. People also become indebted to home mortgages. Much of the "home bubble" crash of 2007-2008 was caused by people who took advantage of the market and let people purchase houses they couldn't afford. Then, the whole economy paid the price for it. Politicians often use debt as a tool to control the masses. The more you get the government's hands out of your business, the better off all of us will be.

So, we have established what the environment was like when these verses were written. This concept of Jubilee as the 50th year is when people are restored. It's a time when people start fresh and new—a clean slate.

I remember taking an introductory psychology course and studying how people approach life. There are theories behind people getting a fresh start—beginning anew. When we come to God, especially through the new birth, bringing that basket load of sin that's destroying us and laying it at the foot of the cross, and we let the blood of Jesus cleanse us from all of it, that's when we get the real clean slate. So, psychology agrees with the Bible that people need a fresh start from time to time. That's what Jubilee does; it gives us a clean slate.

Supernatural debt reduction is sometimes needed to give people a clean start. As a society, we tend to accumulate things. Sometimes, we learn personal economics through our family's foolishness, while some fall to our own chosen behavior.

## RESCUING THE AXE

We find an excellent example of this in 2 Kings:

> And the sons of the prophets said unto Elisha, Behold now, the place where we dwell with thee is too strait for us. Let us go, we pray thee, unto Jordan, and take thence every man a beam, and let us make us a place there, where we may dwell. And he answered, Go ye. And one said, Be content, I pray thee, and go with thy servants. And he answered, I will go. So he went with them. And when they came to Jordan, they cut down wood (2 Kings 6:1-4).

The sons of the prophets were young seminary students studying for the ministry. The word "strait" means *too small.* In other words, the building they were using was getting too small for them to function and do what they needed. So, they came up with an idea for each seminary student to cut a beam. In other words, they are going out to get materials to build a larger school—a larger schoolhouse for the work of the ministry.

"But as one was felling a beam, the ax head fell into the water: and he cried, and said, Alas, master! for it was borrowed" (2 Kings 6:5).

Today, dropping an ax head in the water wouldn't be a momentous event. I've had it happen where the ax head worked itself loose from the handle and came off. I've done enough wood cutting to know that it is more difficult than you might think and requires a certain level of skill. You can easily break the handle if you don't cut wood correctly.

These were seminary students and not woodsmen, so they probably didn't know how to cut wood. Something happened to cause the ax head to end up in the water. Today, we would just go down to a hardware store and purchase another ax. But during that day, these people were under some oppression, so weapons were probably illegal. Plus, iron was not as common as it is today. This ax head was valuable. Losing the ax head is a big thing; it could get someone in serious trouble. This young man trying to get into ministry has no money, and he lost a borrowed ax head. We have a situation that could be potentially problematic.

> And the man of God said, Where fell it? And he showed him the place. And he cut down a

> stick, and cast it in thither; and the iron did swim. Therefore said he, Take it up to thee. And he put out his hand, and took it (2 Kings 6:6-7).

Iron doesn't swim, and it doesn't float. But, in this case, it did. Here we have an illustration of God performing a supernatural, miraculous event to eliminate debt that the borrowed axe created. This is a debt-canceling event through a miracle from a man of God. I'm talking about miracle debt cancellation—not just working hard and getting out of debt. I am talking about a miracle that our debt-canceling God did!

The ax head floated because this young seminary student needed a miracle from God. I'm telling you this by the Spirit of God that if you have college loans, God's miracle-working power is your answer. I speak miracle debt cancellation for you right now, in Jesus' name. That's a specific word for you, not just another verse in the Bible.

## THE OIL

In 2 Kings, chapter 4, we find another example, but first, some backstory. Jezebel was decapitating the prophets. That's a tough place to be. Let's look at 1 Kings 18 for a short backstory:

> And Ahab called Obadiah, which was the governor of his house. (Now Obadiah feared the Lord greatly: For it was so, when Jezebel cut off the prophets of the Lord, that Obadiah took an hundred prophets, and hid them by fifty in a cave, and fed them with bread and water) (1 Kings 18:3-4).

Our story has Obadiah hiding and feeding a hundred prophets who could not go out and work because Jezebel was after them! So, Obadiah risks his life to take care of the prophets.

Now, back to our example in 2 Kings:

> Now there cried a certain woman of the wives of the sons of the prophets unto Elisha, saying, Thy servant my husband is dead; and thou knowest that thy servant did fear the Lord: and the creditor is come to take unto him my two sons to be bondmen (2 Kings 4:1).

Understand that the Bible doesn't say this, but the historian Josephus tells us that the widow mentioned here was probably Obadiah's widow. If this widow woman was Obadiah's wife, she was making a reference to Obadiah. Many believe that the debt she and her sons had was a result of Obadiah hiding the prophets from Jezebel. Again, we don't know that for sure, but it makes sense.

> And Elisha said unto her, What shall I do for thee? tell me, what hast thou in the house? And she said, Thine handmaid hath not any thing in the house, save a pot of oil (2 Kings 4:2).

In other words, the widow was saying, *"We're in debt. My sons are getting ready to be put into bond slavery to pay this debt."* That's her predicament. All she had was a pot of oil. Now, that's abject poverty—miserable, horrible poverty.

> Then he said, Go, borrow thee vessels abroad of all thy neighbours, even empty vessels; borrow not a few. And when thou art come in,

> thou shalt shut the door upon thee and upon thy sons, and shall pour out into all those vessels, and thou shalt set aside that which is full. So she went from him, and shut the door upon her and upon her sons, who brought the vessels to her; and she poured out (2 Kings 4:3-5).

Elisha told her to get every pot, every jar, every pan—everything that would hold liquid. Something was getting ready to happen. So, they started pouring.

> And it came to pass, when the vessels were full, that she said unto her son, Bring me yet a vessel. And he said unto her, There is not a vessel more. And the oil stayed (2 Kings 4:6).

The widow and her sons got every vessel in their village—every vessel they could find that would hold water. They got buckets and tubs; they got it all. She poured from the one pot she had, filling up everything else, and the oil in her pot never went down. It stayed full and filled up all the vessels. Now, look what happened:

> Then she came and told the man of God. And he said, Go, sell the oil, and pay thy debt, and live thou and thy children of the rest (2 Kings 4:7).

When Jesus said, "This day is this Scripture fulfilled in your ears" (Luke 4:21b), He is talking precisely about this right there. He was saying, *"If we can't deliver by normal means, we'll provide by supernatural means. If we can't do it the conventional way, we'll do it the unconventional way. If it takes a miracle, then we'll get one."* I don't know how God can do it, but I know He will—by many or by few. Jesus is our Jubilee. He's our supernatural miracle-working debt-cancelling God.

**If God can't deliver by normal means, He will provide by supernatural means. I don't know how God can, but I know He will.**

God can do for you that which you can't do for yourself, and He's more than willing to do it. He said, *"I am your Jubilee. This day is this Scripture fulfilled in your ears."*

If Jesus did it before, He can do it again. If God did it before, He will do it again. He is the supernatural, miracle-working, debt-cancelling Almighty God. That's who He is, and I'm here to tell you He will do it for you, too.

The prophet asked this little widow, *"What have you got?"* She said, *"I have nothing but a pot of oil."* Elisha said, *"That's enough. Just bring it here."* This question sounds like what God asked Moses, *"What have you got?"* Moses answered, *"I have a stick."* God said, *"I'll take what you have. Just give me what you have, and I'll do for you what you can't do."* God wants to be involved with you. You think you're just in a revolving door and can't ever get out of it, but He wants to get engaged in your life.

**Just give me what you have, and I'll do for you what you can't do.**

## AVOIDING CREDIT

When I was a little boy, my parents would take us to the Sears™ store. All we ever did was use that Sears revolving charge card. You pay the minimum payment and keep going back to Sears. You never managed to pay it in full; everyone always kept paying on their revolving charge cards. I remember when Nora and I made a decision that we would never have a revolving credit account. That was a big deal for us. How are we going to get our back-to-school clothes? Our tires? Our lawnmower? We are going to pay cash. What an amazing concept. God wants you to quit paying minimum payments. He wants to pay off these things for you. We refuse to go into debt for anything now except for maybe a house or car. Eventually, you won't even need to do that. You don't need to go into debt for a vacation.

The highest form of faith is not a higher credit limit. God wants to break the cycle of debt off your life. You have to give Him the pot. Give Him the stick. Give Him something to work with here. Then, cut up your revolving credit cards.

It's a novel concept, paying cash for something. I was somewhere the other day, and the lady asked, *"How do you want to pay?"* I asked her if she took money, and she said yes. Well, that's what I'm going to use. I just want to use cash. Amazing, isn't it? We can become addicted to plastic. I'm not saying anything against it. Use your card; a good credit rating is an asset, but use it the proper way by paying it off at the end of the month.

I'm not getting into debt management in this teaching, but I want you to see that God is a God who can and will supernaturally get you out of debt. It's biblical, and you need to start cooperating with Him. We are talking about supernatural provision.

## HOW DO WE START?

These examples that we covered are about supernatural miracle-working debt cancellation. Jesus is our Jubilee. Well, how do we start? Number one, **you must believe He wants you to be free from debt.** That's where you start. Some people don't believe it; therefore, it will not happen for them. A person may believe, *"I'll never be out of debt."* They probably won't if they think like that.

Next, **you need to see yourself debt-free.** Begin to create an image inside yourself of paying cash. Then, formulate a debt-free strategy as you stop adding more debt. You can't keep accumulating debt if you expect to get out of it. You must also keep sowing seeds. Do your part first before expecting God to do a miracle for you. Remember, satan wants you in debt; he wants to put you in bondage to it. Now is the time for miracle debt cancellation. When we cooperate with God and say what He says, we get what He desires.

What would it feel like to have no mortgage? No car payment? To pay cash for cars? What would having no credit card debt or student loans feel like? What would it be like for you not to borrow for anything? You say, *"Well, could that be?"* Yes, you must begin thinking you can be debt-free because that's where it starts.

Ephesians 3:20 says, "Now unto him that is able to do exceeding abundantly above all that we ask or think, according to **the power** that worketh in us" (emphasis added). What's the power at work in you? It's the power of the Holy Spirit. To what does the Holy Spirit respond? The Spirit of God hovered over the waters, and God **said**, "Let there be light." The Holy

Spirit sprang into action and brought the Word of God to pass. When you get the power of the Word of God working in you by believing the right things, He will do exceedingly, abundantly, beyond, or above all you ask or think according to the power that's working inside you. You start thinking the right things. You start saying the right things. You start doing the right things and watch God do what you can't do. If you can think it up, you can ask it. If you can see it inside you, He will take what's inside you and expand it to levels beyond your ability to comprehend or understand. Let's read that verse from the Amplified Classic:

> Now to Him Who, by (in consequence of) the [action of His] power that is at work within us, is able to [carry out His purpose and] do superabundantly, far over and above all that we [dare] ask or think [infinitely beyond our highest prayers, desires, thoughts, hopes, or dreams]—(Ephesians 3:20, AMPC).

If you can pray it, desire it, think it, hope it, or dream it, God will do better than that. So, if you start thinking that you are debt-free, He said, *"Well, I'll do better than that."* If you will begin to think, *"I can pay cash for a car."* He said, *"I'll do better than that."* He didn't say get a car that will barely get you around. No, God will take you beyond just basic transportation. It's in the Bible; if it offends you, then you have an issue with God.

**God will do infinitely beyond our highest prayers, our highest desires, our highest thoughts, our highest hopes, and our highest dreams.**

I like how ***The Message Bible*** reads:

> God can do anything, you know—far more than you could ever imagine or guess or request in your wildest dreams! He does it not by pushing us around… (Ephesians 3:20, MSG).

Legalists will push you around, condemn you, and tell you why you shouldn't, why you can't, why you don't, and why you won't. God doesn't get you there by pushing you around or condemning you over your mistakes; He works in us. God calls you to want it first. Some may think, *"I can't see any way out of it."* You just have to start seeing it. It's the power that works in you. You get it **inside** you before you can get it on the **outside**.

God, gently and deeply within us, is bringing us into a place of His design. He doesn't want you bound by anything, and that includes debt. Jesus is our Jubilee. He doesn't want you locked down and locked out. The Bible says, "Yea, they turned back and tempted God, and limited the Holy One of Israel" (Psalm 78:41). The Greater One who lives within you doesn't want you bound or limited. God was not pleased with the children of Israel because they limited the Holy One of Israel. Take the limits off.

# 15

# Positioning for Debt Cancellation

In the supernatural realm, there are certain things we need to do to position ourselves for debt cancellation. For example, we know that faith comes by hearing and hearing by the Word of God. In a church, what is taught from the pulpit is manifested in the pew. If you need a move of the Spirit, preach about a move of the Spirit. If you need people to be born again, preach about salvation. A church will get what the pastor preaches because God confirms His Word with signs following the preaching.

Let's look at Colossians 2:

> And you, being dead in your sins and the uncircumcision of your flesh, hath he quickened together with him, having forgiven you all trespasses; Blotting out the handwriting of ordinances that was against us, which was contrary to us, and took it out of the way, nailing it to his cross; (Colossians 2:13-14).

That passage summarizes the whole concept of redemption—Jesus took the note that was written against us. Have you ever heard of a note burning? It's when a church or group of people have worked and labored to pay off a building mortgage and come together to celebrate and burn the note. That is a huge deal to those people. The Bible says there was a note against you. The note against you was the penalty for your sin; a sin debt was levied against us. The Scripture tells us here that not only did Jesus Christ pay the note, but He also destroyed it. He nailed that note to the cross and took it out of the way. So, you're not just forgiven; there's no such thing as a sin debt against you once you come through Jesus Christ.

The New Amplified translation, not the Classic, says it this way:

> Having cancelled out the certificate of debt consisting of legal demands [which were in force] against us and which were hostile to us. And this certificate He has set aside and completely removed by nailing it to the cross (Colossians 2:14, AMP).

Notice what the apostle Paul says here. Jesus canceled out the certificate of debt against us. At its core, the whole concept of the gospel is debt cancelation. Without debt cancelation, you are not saved. So, if you have a debate about whether or not God will cancel your debt, that ought to settle that issue once and for all. The core of the Good News is supernatural debt cancelation—the power of God canceling the debt against us.

I know this refers to sin in that passage, but that's the core of all death with which we deal. I shared this with you earlier, but "mortgage" is a companion word to *mortuary, mortician, and mortality*. It has the concept of death in it. The word "mortgage" means *death grip*, and satan is the author of death.

The whole idea of debt is the squeeze hold that the enemy puts on us because we lack some provision.

Is all debt bad? Some people preach that all debt is a sin, but I don't think it is. It would be better not to have to be in debt. However, in the world we live in, it would be most difficult to live without any form of debt, especially regarding the two big items—our homes and vehicles. In most places, you can't live without a car, especially if you don't have access to mass transportation. So, would I think it's a sin to go into debt for a car? Of course not; it's not a sin. Is it a sin to go into debt for a house? Let me answer that by saying most people would never own a home if they didn't have some amount of debt. Homeownership is also a good form of wealth accumulation for most people. I don't think having a mortgage is a sin, but I think it would be better not to owe.

So, God said He cancelled out the certificate of debt against us. ***The Easy-To-Read Version*** says:

> Because we broke God's laws, we owed a debt—a debt that listed all the rules we failed to follow. But God forgave us of that debt. He took it away and nailed it to the cross (Colossians 2:14, ERV).

God took our debt and canceled it. Again, the debt of sin was nailed to the cross. However, all terrible things and all death emanate from sin. Since mortgages hold a death grip, they have to originate as an outgrowth of sin.

Debt is one of the things satan uses to run our lives and control us. God may lead you to travel to Timbuktu and tell someone about Jesus, but you can't do it if you don't have the money. That is one of the greatest ways that satan restricts us—the lack of financial resources. It's not the only way, but one of the great ways he does it.

The Lord's Prayer is the result of the disciples asking Jesus to teach them to pray. His response is recorded in Matthew 6:

> After this manner therefore pray ye: Our Father which art in heaven, Hallowed be thy name. Thy kingdom come, Thy will be done in earth, as it is in heaven. Give us this day our daily bread. And forgive us our debts, as we forgive our debtors. And lead us not into temptation, but deliver us from evil: For thine is the kingdom, and the power, and the glory, for ever. Amen (Matthew 6:9-13).

This reference is not the only place in the Gospels where the Lord's Prayer is mentioned. Other verses say forgive our trespasses as we forgive those who trespass against us. However, I wanted to point out this passage because Jesus Himself taught us to pray, *"Lord, forgive our debts."* Some may say, *"Well, that just means sin."* Then my question is: Why did He use the word "debt? "Debt" means something that is due or something that is owed. Does it only mean sin or trespass? It does mean that, but it's not isolated to that. I believe that is precisely why the Holy Spirit used that word in the Bible this way. We are told by Jesus Christ, the head of the church, to pray, *"Lord, forgive us our debts."* That is supernatural debt cancellation.

God meant what He said. He is smart. God is not confused. He knows what He meant to say, and He said it the exact way

He wanted it said. Do we believe in the inspiration of Scripture? Do we believe the words that are in the Bible? I believe that if it's in the Bible, we need to read it and do it.

## IT'S CONDITIONAL

Jesus told us to pray, *"Lord, forgive us our debts."* But, there is a qualifier. He said we are to pray, *"Lord, forgive our debts **as we forgive our debtors.**"* To position yourself for supernatural debt cancellation, we must note the qualifier

The Bible is a conditional book. An example of this is found in Isaiah 1:19, which says, "**If you are willing and obedient**, you shall eat the good of the land" (NKJV, emphasis added). So, *"If you are willing and obedient"* precedes *"eat the good of the land."* Whether or not a condition is stated, it's always there. It usually is stated, but if it isn't, you still can't walk in disobedience to God and have the blessing of God. The curse is out there.

It might be said, *"God's cursing people; He's sending a curse."* No, He doesn't have to send anything; it's already cursed. There is a curse of sin on this planet, but Jesus came to redeem us from the curse of the law. However, God does give you an umbrella to use when you go out in the rain. He gives you a shelter from the storm. The Lord gives you something that covers you in the cursed world. However, you can choose to step out of the blessing and into the curse by putting down that umbrella. So, get under the umbrella.

When it's raining, I use an umbrella to take my dog out. The umbrella is there to protect me from the elements. God has given us protection—a covering—and a shield of defense against the curse. All you have to do to go back under the curse is forget the umbrella. You get wet without an umbrella; that's just the way it is. Get under the covering.

**God gives you a shelter from the storm—an umbrella to use when you go out in the rain. To step out of the blessing and into the curse, just put down the umbrella.**

Some people get confused and blame God for their troubles. However, they must realize that He didn't send or do anything. The curse is already here. If you read Deuteronomy 28 closely, you find that all the blessings come on you and overtake you **if you hearken unto the voice of the Lord**. But if you don't, it gives a long list of curses. The curse exists; sickness, poverty, torment, sadness, and lost joy are under the curse. All you have to do is put down the umbrella, and the curse is there. It's not God doing it; it's something that already exists, but God gives us protection from that curse.

## INTEGRITY OF HEART

Jesus taught us, "Forgive us our debts, as we forgive our debtors" (Matthew 6:12). He told us to pray that, but let's go on down where He said:

> For if ye forgive men their trespasses, your heavenly Father will also forgive you: But if ye forgive not men their trespasses, neither will your Father forgive your trespasses (Matthew 6:14-15).

Notice that these verses put "trespass" in the category of "debt." Debt means something owed or something that's due. We understand that the sin debt is the core or the greatest debt. The sin debt is the one Jesus took and nailed to the cross. So, debt forgiveness is what the gospel is all about. Everything hinges on that.

Debt is a part of business and life. In other words, if people owe you in the course of your business, they are indebted to you. That's cash flow or cash movement, which is part of doing business. So, when we talk about God wanting you out of debt, that is not an excuse for not paying your debts. There are Bible ways of doing things, and that's not one of them.

Romans 13:8 says, "Owe no man any thing, but to love one another." That means if you owe no one anything, you've already paid them. In other words, if you owe someone, go ahead and pay them and get that debt off the books. You don't owe them because you have already paid them. Someone said, *"Well, I don't use credit cards."* We use credit cards all the time, but we pay them off at the end of the month. When you accumulate the result of your spending, then pay it. Some people don't want to pay their bills, but they want the stuff. If you have credit cards, just pay them at the end of the month.

In 2 Corinthians 8, it says:

> "Providing for honest things, not only in the sight of the Lord, but also in the sight of men."

We must be honest people. If we make a debt, pay it. You are not entitled to a reprieve of what you owe just because you are believing God to reduce your debt—not at someone else's expense. That's not the way He does it.

Psalm 15:4 says, "In whose eyes a vile person is contemned; but he honoureth them that fear the Lord. He that sweareth to his own hurt, and changeth not." When you give your word, you're stuck with it. The Bible says you swear to your own hurt and change not. If you have no integrity, you're a deadbeat, and it doesn't matter. If you are a child of God and you have some integrity of heart about you, it does matter—a great deal. So, we are not entitled to make debts and not pay them.

## LENDING TO FAMILY & FRIENDS

In business, we work on credit or time. People may owe for work performed, and then they are supposed to pay for it. The terms may be 30, 60, or 90 days, but it's paid when it's time to pay it. However, dealing with family and friends is different.

Personally, I don't think you should loan money to family. I don't think you should because of two big reasons: Christmas and Thanksgiving. If you still want peaceful family get-togethers, don't loan money to your family. If you do, make sure it's money you can afford to lose. Lending money you can't afford to lose is unwise. With family, if you have discretionary money, just give it to them and forget about it. It takes everyone off the hook.

Let's go back to Matthew 6 in the Amplified Version.

> "'And forgive us our debts, as we have forgiven our debtors [letting go of both the wrong and the resentment]'" (Matthew 6:12, AMP).

If you lend money to family or friends, you are getting ready to have some issues. A friend of mine provided a regular service to some people who accumulated a sizable tab, but the people left town without paying. You trust people, but you may end up in that situation.

You just can't hold on to a breach of trust for 20 years. This verse is not talking about the regular ebb and flow of business; it's talking about those who don't pay when they should. Notice that the Amplified Version says, "'*Letting go of both the wrong and the resentment.*'" You are better off to let these things go because you will not get the money anyway. A person can hold it and harbor resentment almost to the point where you get hateful about it and still won't get the money. Thirty years is too long to keep these grudges. This stuff breeds family feuds and parts the best of friends.

Debt among family members can generate great strife and division. They will pay everyone on the planet except you. You are the only one that can't send a collection agency. They are not paying you. I think it's better to forgive the debt than to destroy the relationship.

Jesus was telling us to forgive so we don't hold on to the wrongs and resentment. When we forgive a debt and let go of the wrong, we loose the things holding on to us, not them. So, we let it go. Some people use debt to control. You've seen parents loan money to their kids so they can control their lives—run their marriages. They use it for leverage or as a tool to gain an advantage. They use it to hold something over another's head. No, no, no.

Matthew 6 from the Amplified Classic says it this way:

> And forgive us our debts, as we also have forgiven (left, remitted, and let go of the debts and have given up resentment against) our debtors (Matthew 6:12, AMPC).

You've got to give up resentment. ***The Common English Bible*** says:

> "Forgive us the ways we have wronged you,
> just as we also forgive those who have wronged us"
> (Matthew 6:12, CEB).

## APPEAL TO PHILEMON

We are talking about supernatural debt cancellation, but it goes back to Calvary, the cross, and taking away the note against us because all debt emanates from the result of the devil's work on this planet. Without his work, we wouldn't have any debt because God has provided. The Garden of Eden shows us that there was no need for debt. There was plenty of provision there.

However, there are times when people have no ability to pay. For example, we find this story in the book of Philemon. It's an important story to illustrate this concept of debt reduction or supernatural debt cancellation. Here's the backstory on Paul's letter to Philemon:

Philemon had a slave named Onesimus, who apparently ran away. Legally, he couldn't do that because Onesimus was recognized as real property belonging to Philemon, just like a home or other equipment—it was slavery. It was customary in that day and time; no one condones it, but that's how it was. If Onesimus was found, he could have been imprisoned or returned to his master. Since he broke the law, he's a criminal on the run because he escaped without being released.

Now, we pick up this story in Philemon, chapter 1, with the apostle Paul writing to Philemon, saying, "I beseech thee for my son Onesimus, whom I have begotten in my bonds:" (Philemon 1:10). So, Onesimus ran away, but while running, he got saved. When Paul was in prison, somehow, he led this slave to the Lord. Paul wrote a letter to Philemon on behalf of Onesimus' predicament because they knew each other. Let's walk through this passage of Scripture.

> Which in time past was to thee unprofitable, but now profitable to thee and to me: Whom I have sent again: thou therefore receive him, that is, mine own bowels: (Philemon 1:11-12).

In other words, Onesimus wasn't doing Philemon any good the way he was, but now he's profitable to both Paul and Philemon. Paul was sending a letter of endorsement to Philemon, on behalf of Onesimus, to forgive him. Onesimus is a slave and highly indebted with no ability to pay. He can't even get a job. It continues:

> Whom I would have retained with me, that in thy stead he might have ministered unto me in the bonds of the gospel: But without thy mind would I do nothing; that thy benefit should not be as it were of necessity, but willingly. For perhaps he therefore departed for a season, that thou shouldest receive him for ever; (Philemon 1:13-15).

Paul was saying, *"I'd like Onesimus to stay with me, but I'm not going to do anything without your approval and permission. We don't know all the circumstances, Philemon. Maybe the devil was at work here. But whatever the case may be, when he left, he got saved. Now you're getting someone else back; you're getting a new creature back."*

> Not now as a servant, but above a servant, a brother beloved, specially to me, but how much more unto thee, both in the flesh, and in the Lord? If thou count me therefore a partner, receive him as myself. If he hath wronged thee, or oweth thee ought, put that on mine account; (Philemon 1:16-18).

Paul told Philemon that Onesimus left him as a servant and is returning as a brother. Then, Paul says, *"If he owes you anything, I'll pay you."* He's talking about physical money here; he wasn't just talking about owing in the spirit. We're seeing debt cancellation here. That is what Jesus conveyed when He said, *"You forgive them as I have forgiven you. You canceled their debt just like I canceled your debt."* Let's continue and see how Paul qualifies it a bit. He said:

> I Paul have written it with mine own hand, I will repay it: albeit I do not say to thee how thou owest unto me even thine own self besides (Philemon 1:19).

Paul was saying, *"I signed it right here. I'll pay it. My word is on this."* Now, this is the qualifier, he said, *"I'll pay his debt, but remember this: you owe me your life."* Yes, it's spiritual; it was nailed to the cross. Our sins are taken out of the way. But here's a man that's going to debtor's prison if someone doesn't take up for him.

The point here is that Jesus—*Jehovah Jireh*—is taking up for you. He is taking your case. We are not talking about deadbeats who won't pay their bills and use the Bible as an excuse. We are not talking about a business structure that uses 60 or 90-day credits. However, we are talking about someone who has no ability to pay, and without someone stepping in, they are going to jail. That's serious stuff right there.

## FORGIVENESS IS A MUST

We just keep grinding away at that debt; the mill keeps grinding the corn. God wants you out of debt, and He's willing to get you there. Someone may say, *"I don't know if He can get me there."* Well, I don't think you're any worse off than Onesimus; he was in a bad predicament! Here's the account of Jesus teaching in Matthew 18:

> Therefore is the kingdom of heaven likened unto a certain king, which would take account of his servants. And when he had begun to reckon, one was brought unto him, which owed him ten thousand talents (Matthew 18:23-24).

The king we know is the Father. The servants would be those in His Kingdom; in typology, that would be us. Talents represent money. So, one of His servants came to Him with a heavy bondage of debt. Let's look at the following verses:

> But forasmuch as he had not to pay, his lord commanded him to be sold, and his wife, and children, and all that he had, and payment to be

> made. The servant therefore fell down, and worshipped him, saying, Lord, have patience with me, and I will pay thee all. Then the lord of that servant was moved with compassion, and loosed him, and forgave him the debt (Matthew 18:25-27).

In other words, he owed a debt he couldn't pay. We don't have a debtor's prison, but they did. His family lost everything they had, and all of them were put into servitude. That's a pretty severe debt—a debt way beyond the pale. The rest of this passage illustrates what happened at Calvary to each of us. The servant fell down and worshipped, and the lord forgave him. The Lord forgave the truckload of debt we threw at the foot of the cross; His blood washed it away. We had a debt we couldn't pay, but Jesus paid the price and forgave the debt.

> But the same servant went out, and found one of his fellowservants, which owed him an hundred pence went out, and found one of his fellowservants, which owed him an hundred pence: and he laid hands on him, and took him by the throat, saying, Pay me that thou owest. And his fellowservant fell down at his feet, and besought him, saying, Have patience with me, and I will pay thee all. And he would not: but went and cast him into prison, till he should pay the debt. So when his fellowservants saw what was done, they were very sorry, and came and told unto their lord all that was done. Then his lord, after that he had called him, said unto him, O thou wicked servant, I forgave thee all that debt, because thou desiredst me: (Matthew 18:28-32).

The servant himself owed a massive debt, but someone else owed him a minor debt. That's when we pray, "Lord, forgive my debts as I forgive my debtors."

> Shouldest not thou also have had compassion on thy fellowservant, even as I had pity on thee? And his lord was wroth, and delivered him to the tormentors, till he should pay all that was due unto him (Matthew 18:33-34).

Remember what we read in Matthew 6:12 from the Amplified Bible: We must let go of the wrong, the resentment, and the torment attached to holding debt. You let it go. It's much better for you to let it go than to hold it. Reading on in this passage:

> And his lord was wroth, and delivered him to the tormentors, till he should pay all that was due unto him. So likewise shall my heavenly Father do also unto you, if ye from your hearts forgive not every one his brother their trespasses (Matthew 18:34-35).

If we position ourselves for supernatural debt cancellation and supernatural debt reduction, we have to be willing to forgive people who need to be forgiven. Of course, it means forgiveness of sin, but it may include forgiveness of a monetary issue. There are times when you need to let it go. They are not going to pay you any quicker just because you harbor it—just because you hold on to it. Sometimes, when we release it, it releases us.

These things are how you get positioned for the release of heaven into your life. Let it go. Give it up. Now, I'm not talking about business; I'm not talking about forgiving every debt. I'm talking about when there is no ability to pay and no ability to do anything; just let it go. When dealing with family who owes you, just drop it because you need Christmas and Thanksgiving back.

## THE PROMISE

God told me, ***"If you teach how to position yourself for supernatural debt cancellation, and they do it, it will open up the floodgates of heaven into their lives."*** You haven't seen anything yet, but you're getting ready to see miraculous things.

Look at Matthew 6:12 again, which says, "And forgive us our debts, as we have forgiven our debtors [letting go of both the wrong and the resentment]" (AMP). Let it go. Let it go. Let it go. That same Jesus who took our sin debt and nailed it to the cross, spoke these words. We could not be more Christlike than forgiving those who have no way to repay and cannot do anything good for you. Just let it go. In letting it go, you will open the power of God into your life in ways you have never ever imagined. He will do things for you beyond your wildest dreams and beyond your wildest imaginations. For example, you could be trying to sell something, and you haven't had a bite on it in over ten years. Then, bam, it sells the very next day. That's not just a coincidence.

The Lord is saying:

> *Do you not know who Jehovah Jireh is? Do you not know, saith the Lord, the things that I can do on behalf of you? Do you not know who I am, saith the Lord? Do you not know My abilities? And even more, not only do you not know My abilities, do you not know My willingness and My desire to move on your behalf, saith the Lord?*

# 16

# Prioritizing the Lord's Work

In the last chapter, we talked about positioning ourselves for supernatural and miracle debt cancellation. This chapter covers part two of the story. Remember, there are ways to which we must adhere to get in position to receive from the Lord. Positioning is essential as we prepare to receive. The Bible says, "But as many as **received** Him, to them gave he power to become the sons of God" (John 1:12, emphasis added). Over and over, the Bible talks about receiving. It says you must believe that you **receive** when you pray, and then you will **receive** that for which you pray.

As a preamble, let's consider the Super Bowl and the fanatical football enthusiasts it attracts. One of the positions we spotlight extensively on a team is the wide receiver—someone whose primary responsibility is to catch passes. To do that job well, they must put themselves in a position to be able to receive or catch the ball. Outmaneuvering the defender is tantamount to the receiving process. And so, we understand what is meant by "receiving" when we put it in that category.

In the same way, when you receive from God, you must also put yourself in a position to receive. There is an opponent, the same as in a football game, who wants to thwart your ability to receive. That opponent is your adversary, the devil. We can overcome him, but we must do it on purpose by positioning ourselves to receive.

As we go through this study on supernatural or miracle debt cancellation, I want to emphasize prioritizing the Lord's work or the Lord's house. In the context of supernatural or miracle debt cancellation, it is a great part of positioning ourselves to receive.

Let's look at Matthew 6:

> What shall we drink? or, Wherewithal shall we be clothed? (For after all these things do the Gentiles seek:) for your heavenly Father knoweth that ye have need of all these things. But seek ye first the kingdom of God, and his righteousness; and all these things shall be added unto you (Matthew 6:31-33).

We take thoughts by saying them. That's how you take a thought—you say it, agree with it, or dwell on it much too long. This verse is talking about provision, food, and clothing. When Jesus tells us to "seek first," He's talking about priorities.

Sometimes, we have a propensity to get *hyper-spiritual* in a general sense. We sing songs like "Jesus is All I Need." It sounds great and everything, but the problem is that it's not really true. Jesus is the great *"Need Meeter,"* but He's not all you need. There are other things that you definitely need, including, but not limited to, shelter, food, clothing, and transportation. We need some things to live this life, and God says He has given us all things that pertain to life and godliness (2 Peter 1:3). So, He will provide both the spiritual and the natural.

We must prioritize the kingdom of God. The word "kingdom" is a combination of two words: "king" and "dominion"—the dominion of the king—King Jesus and His Lordship over circumstance and things. So, when we seek His Kingdom first, the kingdom of God, all these things it takes to live a natural life can and shall be added to us.

The Scripture says we humans tend to let things slip (Hebrews 2:1). These "things" have been a part of our lives at one time, but we go on with other things and even look at the Scriptures from different vantage points. Then, those things that were once common knowledge to us begin to slip because we don't keep reminding ourselves of them.

The Bible also talks about when you have a supper and bid people to come—a type and a reference of inviting people to the marriage supper of the Lamb (Luke 14:16-20). This passage says those who were bidden began with "one consent to make excuse" about attending the supper. In other words, *"I don't have time to do the things that would give me entrance to the marriage supper."* This passage ends by mentioning family, work, personal interests, property, and things that can get in the way of serving God.

I am sometimes amused by people who can get off track so easily. This observation is not because it's funny, but it's something so clearly wrong that it is amusing that it would be so easy to get people off track. You would think the devil wouldn't have it so easy.

You can watch people and the priorities they put on things that don't mean anything. I wouldn't give the souls of my kids to a soccer coach, no matter how accomplished; I would give them to the church. If they were on a soccer team that was constantly and unapologetically in conflict with the church, I'd find another team. Your child is not going to heaven because they play soccer. Some run all over creation after a sport and can't even bring their children to a youth group. Then we wonder why they grow up not knowing anything about Jesus Christ. The world gets them all day, every day, and you should at least be able to give them two hours a week in church. But I'm a pastor, and the Lord requires me to help people see where their priorities belong.

Our key passage of Scripture helps us with our priorities. Jesus said:

> But **seek ye first** the kingdom of God, and His righteousness; and all these things shall be added unto you. Take therefore no thought for the morrow; for the morrow shall take thought for the things of itself. Sufficient unto the day is the evil thereof (Matthew 6:33-34, emphasis added).

## WHEN GOD SENDS SOMEONE

There is a story in 1 Kings 17 that illustrates prioritizing the kingdom of God quite graphically:

> And the word of the Lord came unto [the prophet], saying, Arise, get thee to Zarephath, which belongeth to Zidon, and dwell there: behold, I have commanded a widow woman there to sustain thee (1 Kings 17:8-9, emphasis added).

In this passage, God had spoken to a widow woman, but she had not heard Him. She evidently was not sensitive enough to hear Him, or her circumstances clouded His voice. Sometimes, we can even tell ourselves, *"God couldn't be talking to me about this."* Conditioned responses can stop us from hearing the voice of the Lord.

Some say, *"I don't believe God speaks anyway."* Well, the book of Revelation says something completely different, so that could be a problem. The Lord said, "Behold, I stand at the door, and knock: if any man **hear my voice**, and open the door, I will come in to him, and will sup with him, and he with me" (Revelation 3:20, emphasis added). Therefore, any man can hear Him. He speaks to everyone. God is talking all the time; it's us who aren't listening.

Let's get back to our story in 1 Kings:

> So he arose and went to Zarephath. And when he came to the gate of the city, behold, the widow woman was there gathering of sticks: and he called to her, and said, Fetch me, I pray thee, a little water in a vessel, that I may drink. And as she was going to fetch it, he called to her, and said, Bring me, I pray thee, a morsel of bread in thine hand. And she said, As the Lord thy God liveth, I have not a cake, but an handful of meal in a barrel, and a little oil in a cruse: and, behold, I am gathering two sticks, that I may go in and dress it for me and my son, that we may eat it, and die (1 Kings 17:10-12).

Without a doubt, this woman was in dire circumstances. At least in her eyes, if she and her son didn't have some form of intervention, they were looking at their absolute last morsel. They had come to their final meal.

> And Elijah said unto her, Fear not; go and do as thou hast said: but make me thereof a little cake first, and bring it unto me, and after make for thee and for thy son (1 Kings 17:13).

The prophet's words wouldn't fly well in today's news media with the disparaging things they say about preachers. Elijah told her, "Make me a little cake first." The point here is not giving to the man of God. We're not talking about the subject of ministerial support; we're talking about the priority of the kingdom of God. The prophet represented God to this woman. For our understanding, he represents everything related to God. This passage is talking about seeking first the Kingdom. This man went down there and gave the woman an up close and personal way of seeking God's Kingdom first. He had to draw her out of her dire circumstances and her own thinking. The prophet was saying, *"You don't have to die here. Change your thought process."*

Furthermore, he wasn't telling her to take the cake down to the corner church. He was saying, "We have to do this now, and we have to do it right here." Elijah knew she would not have followed through if he left her to her own devices. So, he somewhat had to push the issue because it's serious business. We are talking about life and death in the literal sense. So, he said, *"Make me a little cake first and bring it to me, and after you've done that, make one for you and your son."* He is helping her prioritize the Kingdom.

Remember, our subject is positioning yourself for supernatural debt cancellation. If you prioritize debt, you'll probably have to live in it. I've heard some say, *"Okay, I'll give to the work of the Lord as soon as I get my bills paid and as soon as I get out of this hole."* I've found over the years that money managers will tell people in a debt crisis or with money management issues to quit giving. They advise you to pay your debts, and then you can give. Biblically, that is as wrong as it gets and poor advice. You get no supernatural, divine help if you follow that pathway. God won't intervene if you follow that path. You must prioritize the kingdom of God if you want God's assistance in helping you relinquish, liquidate, or get out of debt. We have to put God's Kingdom first.

So, Elijah said to make him a cake first and then:

> For thus saith the Lord God of Israel, The barrel of meal shall not waste, neither shall the cruse of oil fail, until the day that the Lord sendeth rain upon the earth. And she went and did according to the saying of Elijah: and she, and he, and her house, did eat many days. And the barrel of meal wasted not, neither did the cruse of oil fail, according to the word of the Lord, which he spake by Elijah (1 Kings 17:14-16).

When the widow did what the prophet said, she got the results that the prophet said would come. When you do what the Word of God says, you'll get what the Word of God says in your life. It's interesting because this was a recognized prophet, and he had all the signs of a prophet in his life and ministry. With that in mind, look in 2 Chronicles 20:

> And they rose early in the morning, and went forth into the wilderness of Tekoa: and as they went forth, Jehoshaphat stood and said, Hear me, O Judah, and ye inhabitants of Jerusalem; Believe in the LORD your God, so shall ye be established; **believe his prophets, so shall ye prosper** (2 Chronicles 20:20, emphasis added).

Sometimes, God will send you someone to tell you something. However, if you don't believe them, then you're going to have a hard time getting what God wanted you to have.

A person may say, *"I believe the Bible and only the Bible."* Then, they are out of order. You are supposed to believe the Bible, but the Bible says if you receive a prophet in the name of a prophet, you'll receive the prophet's reward (Matthew 10:41). God will send you someone to tell you how to do what you need to do, and you need to listen to them.

Another person may say, *"I don't listen to just anybody."* Again, you are out of order because the Bible says that both stubbornness and rebellion are sins. So, God sends you someone, and you say, *"Well, I don't want that person. I want God to send me someone else."* Okay, but that's what Naaman the Syrian said. If he had refused to listen to what the prophet told him, he would have died of leprosy (2 Kings 5). God is not going to qualify who He sends to you. He will send you whom He chooses, and it's your job to pay attention.

Then, someone adds, *"But I don't want to listen."* Yes, I know. Just like every other human on the planet, we don't want to listen to anyone. That kind of behavior is not the God-nature in us; it's our human nature that springs forth from pride. It takes work to listen and respond.

Let's look at this verse in 2 Chronicles again, but this time from the New International Version. The latter part says, "Have faith in the Lord your God and you will be upheld; have faith in his prophets and you will be successful" (2 Chronicles 20:20, NIV). That's a good promise. God reveals here that He wants you to be successful, but He's going to send you someone to tell you how to prosper.

Some people may not like the word "prosperity," but the Bible is jam-packed full of it. People can use many experiences to illustrate prosperity, both good and bad, but you just have to believe the Bible. **Your faith does not stand in the wisdom of man but in the power of God.** You can't qualify your faith through someone's experience that you don't know behind the scenes. You don't know what kind of lifestyle they're living or anything else about them. You don't know all the details of their life, so you can't judge things based solely on outward appearances.

## GOD'S STANDARDS

God's dealings with man changed at Calvary. Jesus, the Lamb slain before the foundation of the world, was not an afterthought to God. In the sequence or fullness of time, God sent His Son to be born of a woman. So, time elevated how He dealt with man to another level. We are under grace now, but the Old Testament was under the Law. Even then, God knew Jesus was coming; He still was working His plan. A day is coming when we step out of this flesh and go to the other side, which will bring on another dispensation of God's dealing with humanity that is different from today.

There's an account in Ezekiel chapter 44 that provides a synopsis of the priesthood. When it talks about the priesthood, it details specific duties and behaviors for those in that position. In the New Testament, we don't look at the priesthood like they did under the Old Covenant, so we're not trying to overlay all this behavior, conduct, or comportment into the New Testament. However, in principle, God still looks at humanity through the same eyes. There is no variableness nor shadow of turning in Him. He is the same yesterday, today, and forever. He does not change, but **how He deals with us does change.**

Ezekiel chapter 44 talks about how Old Testament priests were supposed to dress, among other things:

> And it shall come to pass, that when they enter in at the gates of the inner court, they shall be clothed with linen garments; and no wool shall come upon them, whiles they minister in the gates of the inner court, and within. They shall have linen bonnets upon their heads, and shall have linen breeches upon their loins; they shall not gird themselves with any thing that causeth sweat. And when they go forth into the utter court, even into the utter court to the people, they shall put off their garments wherein they ministered, and lay them in the holy chambers, and they shall put on other garments; and they shall not sanctify the people with their garments. Neither shall they shave their heads, nor suffer their locks to grow long; they shall only poll their heads (Ezekiel 44:17-20).

The priests were to dress in certain garments and present themselves in specific ways. Verse 21 goes on to say that they can't drink any wine. The following verses say who they can and cannot marry. They were supposed to teach certain things and present sin offerings. There were just a lot of rules. We have more leeway than they did because we are under grace, but my point is that God has some standards. Let's continue reading these rules:

> And they shall teach my people the difference between the holy and profane, and cause them to discern between the unclean and the clean. And in controversy they shall stand in judgment; and they shall judge it according to my judgments: and they shall keep my laws and my statutes in all mine assemblies; and they shall hallow my sabbaths. And they shall come at no dead person to defile themselves: but for father, or for mother, or for son, or for daughter, for brother, or for sister that hath had no husband, they may defile themselves. And after he is cleansed, they shall reckon unto him seven days. And in the day that he goeth into the sanctuary, unto the inner court, to minister in the sanctuary, he shall offer his sin offering, saith the Lord God. And it shall be unto them for an inheritance: **I am their inheritance: and ye shall give them no possession in Israel: I am their possession** (Ezekiel 44:23-28, emphasis added).

When God meted out the land to the people—the tribe of Benjamin gets this portion, and the tribe of Naphtali gets that portion—the tribe of Levi, where the priests came from, received no inheritance. They didn't get any land. It seems unfair that the priests didn't inherit any possessions, but they could not be involved in buying, selling, and doing everyday things because they were dedicated to the work of the Lord.

So, they didn't get that physical inheritance. So, God said, *"I'll be their inheritance."* Therefore, the other tribes were to support the Levites. God gave specific guidelines for the support of the ministry. He gave the tribes the responsibility to care for the priests because they couldn't be involved in monetary exchange like everyone else. They had to see to it that the Levites were cared for properly.

The next verse says, "They shall eat the meat offering, and the sin offering, and the trespass offering: and every dedicated thing in Israel shall be theirs" (Ezekiel 44:29). Certain things were brought into the house of the Lord. It wasn't there for everyone, but it was there for the priests. Then, we read:

> And the first of all the firstfruits of all things, and every oblation of all, of every sort of your oblations, shall be the priest's: ye shall also give unto the priest the first of your dough, **that he may cause the blessing to rest in thine house** (Ezekiel 44:30, emphasis added).

The priesthood support does not work that way now, but it still requires us to take care of the preacher—the principle crosses over. The "dough" mentioned here is not talking about money, and we're not talking about ministerial support but illustrating a principle that's the focus of our study. We are talking about positioning ourselves for supernatural debt cancellation or miracle debt cancellation and the priority of the Kingdom as it relates to that.

Again, Proverbs says, "The blessing of the Lord, it maketh rich, and he addeth no sorrow with it" (Proverbs 10:22). You don't need a modern translation to understand that; it's straightforward. If you are going to have any supernatural provision, it's going to come because the Lord blesses your life. It will not come because of any other reason. It comes from the blessing of the Lord.

I learned this from a true man of God. He is wealthy beyond measure—one of the richest men in the world. I saw the abundance of things God brought to him, and his response to it was only to recognize God's goodness. He never took credit for any of it. We discussed how God had done things in his life—taking him from being broke to being rich. It was a true rags-to-riches story. He started with less than nothing, being illiterate. God saved him and took him step-by-step and made him a billionaire. He always said God's goodness took him to that place. That should be your statement as well. Any time God does something for you, it should be credited to God's goodness. If people say, *"Well, aren't you smart."* God's goodness. *"How did you get there?"* God's goodness. *"Well, how did you get that?"* God's goodness. It's always God's goodness. That attitude keeps you from getting into pride. It keeps you from being lifted up. The blessing of the Lord is going to get you that miracle debt cancellation that you need.

Let's go back to the latter part of Ezekiel 44:30, which says, "That he may cause the blessing to rest in thine house." God told us to give to the priests first. For our purposes, we will call it "the Kingdom" because we are to seek first the Kingdom. The priest was a representative of God's Kingdom, like Elijah was a representative of the Kingdom. Ezekiel says to give the priest the first of your dough so that he may cause the blessing to rest in thine house.

In other words, putting the Kingdom first brings the blessing to rest in your house. I don't know if that means anything to you, but that means everything to me. When you can get God camped out with you, your lifestyle is getting ready to improve. Things are getting ready to perk up around your house. When God comes to stay in your home, He has a lifestyle that's bigger than yours, and He is going to let you live it with Him. You have no idea what can begin to happen when God takes up residence in your life through His blessing coming to rest in your house. By the way, **it is that blessing that makes you rich and provides everything you need** because "the blessing of the Lord, it maketh rich" (Proverbs 10:22).

**When God comes to stay at your home, He has a lifestyle that is bigger than yours, and He is going to let you live it with Him.**

When the blessing rests at your house, you won't be living from paycheck to paycheck, disaster to disaster, peak to peak, just trudging through the valleys. There will be plenty to make the valleys high and the mountains low. He's going to make your future like a level plain. You won't be wondering where it's coming from. You will have more than enough, and you won't even know the lean times from the high times because there is so much it won't matter. *"What if the car breaks down?"* Fix it! *"What if the heat and air unit stops working?"* Fix it! There's never a crisis because it's only a crisis when you can't manage it. God does not want you to live from emergency to emergency; He has a better way of doing things.

Do you know the old saying, *"Robbing Peter to pay Paul?"* First of all, you didn't need to rob either one to pay the other because they were both wealthy. The archeological record shows that Peter had the largest house in the town where he lived. Peter said, "Silver and gold have I none," (Acts 3:6) which may have been the case at that moment in time, but it didn't stay that way.

## GIVING A GIFT

Let's look at Matthew 5:

> Therefore if thou bring thy gift to the altar, and there rememberest that thy brother hath ought against thee; Leave there thy gift before the altar, and go thy way; first be reconciled to thy brother, and then come and offer thy gift (Matthew 5:23-24).

First, we bring our gift to the altar. That's important since we are talking about making God's Kingdom our first priority. In prioritizing the Kingdom, we bring our gift to the altar. When you see the word "altar" in the Bible, it's a place where God and man have some form of exchange notable enough to remember.

Moses had a burning bush. It was such a notable event in the desert that they heaped rocks to remember it. It wasn't a temple; it was a pile of rocks—an altar—placed there so Moses wouldn't forget where it happened. It was done so he could return and honor the principle or the process that took place at that point in his life.

The altar becomes sacred because other people also recognize it. Then, you build a temple over a heap of rocks. If you go to the Holy Land, they construct temples over rock piles because they don't want to forget. If you go to where Jesus was born, a big church is built over it now. The church protects it and enshrines the sacredness of the event.

**An altar is a place where God and man have a memorable exchange.**

In the New Testament, we have a church and a sanctuary. The word "sanctuary" means a sanctified place set apart for the work of God. In the sanctuary, we have an altar, not to be confused with a stage as we know it. The altar is where exchanges take place—where God visits you, where He talks to you, where you come and bring your needs, and where business between God and man happens. It's a place of business. Holy business. Kingdom business.

So, we bring our gifts to the altar, and we have an exchange. We are saying, *"I honor you, Lord. I bring you a gift out of honor and respect. I lay it on the altar."* That's what an offering is. An offering can't be **taken**; it must be **given**. A church can't "take" an offering; it doesn't qualify as an offering if you have to take it. You "give" an offering.

Out of respect, we bring to God something valuable to us because He's valuable to us. We honor Him with our giving. We love Him; we respect Him. We want to see His name exalted. We want to see His Kingdom expand. Therefore, we become participants in it through our giving. We bring our gifts to the altar.

## HONOR THE ALTAR

Let's go to Matthew 23, which says, "Ye fools and blind: for whether is greater, the gold, or the temple that sanctifieth the gold? And, Whosoever shall swear by the altar, it is nothing;" (Matthew 23:17-18). These verses reference the temple of Jesus' day.

There's an entire backstory to this Bible passage. People had been acting as if it didn't matter if you swear by the altar, but you better not swear by the gold on the altar. In other words, their mistaken priority elevated the gold on the altar.

So, Jesus gives perspective on what they were doing that brought dishonor. The people were dishonoring the temple—the house of God, but they honored the things in it. They honored money, but they didn't esteem the work. They revered the money but didn't honor the souls saved at that altar. That's what religion can do to you. That is the context of what's going on here. Jesus was saying, *"You don't care about the altar, but you swear by the money on it."* The temple is over the altar, and the altar is the place where the exchange takes place, but you honor what is put on the altar, and you don't esteem everything else. You must honor the God of heaven. You need to honor the altar—the house of God.

This thought goes back to when you bring your gift to the altar, as we read in Matthew 5, which is saying, *"Bring your gift to the altar, but if you have a brother with something against you, go get it straight."* We can be guilty of honoring the gift while not honoring what makes the gift work. We must honor the spirit behind it.

Jesus puts our giving or offering in the context of being something extraordinarily spiritual. We must remember the spiritual part of it. We can't forget the spiritual part. That's what He is talking about here. Jesus goes on to issue a warning to beware of thinking that what's laid on the altar is more important than the altar.

Let's continue to read in Matthew:

"Ye fools and blind: for whether is greater,
the gift, or the altar that sanctifieth the gift?"
(Matthew 23:19).

Jesus was saying, *"If you put money out on the curb, it's the same money; it means nothing in a spiritual context. However, when you lay the gift on the altar, it changes."* **Money doesn't change the altar; the altar changes the money.** Our gift turns into a sacred thing. It wasn't sacred lying on the curb; it's not sacred until someone puts it into God's hands.

Prioritizing God's house—God's Kingdom—opens you up to the provision of God. When we bring the "dough" first (as we talked about in Ezekiel 44), it causes the blessing to rest on the house. It is the blessing that makes you rich or brings His provision to you. Let's look at this verse from the New Living Translation:

"How blind! For which is more important—
the gift on the altar or the altar that makes the gift sacred?"
(Matthew 23:19, NLT).

It's the altar that makes the gift sacred. For example, when you put your tithe or offering into the Kingdom, the remaining amount in your bank account has the blessing on it. When you bring your gift first, then what is left has a blessing on it. Jesus was saying, *"I'll put the blessing in your house to stay, not to come and go, but to come and stay."*

## THE GOAL IN GIVING

Let's stay in Matthew 23 and read an upcoming verse:

> Woe unto you, scribes and Pharisees, hypocrites! for ye pay tithe of mint and anise and cummin, and have omitted the weightier matters of the law, judgment, mercy, and faith: **these ought ye to have done**, and not to leave the other undone (Matthew 23:23, emphasis added).

Jesus was saying, *"You are so strict with the tithe that you even tithe spices, but you don't forgive your brother. You are legalistic about the tithe but omit the weightier matters."*

Is Jesus saying the tithe doesn't matter—just forgive everyone? No. He said, *"These ought ye to have done."* In other words, it's good for you to tithe on the spice; you should do that. However, you must also forgive.

Someone may say, *"I don't believe tithing is New Testament."* Jesus Christ, the head of the Church, said we ought to tithe. What are we going to do about that?

Let us explore Malachi chapter three. You will find that verses one and two talk about the first and second coming of Jesus. It says:

> Behold, I will send my messenger, and he shall prepare the way before me: and the Lord, whom ye seek, shall suddenly come to his temple, even the messenger of the covenant, whom ye delight

> in: behold, he shall come, saith the Lord of hosts. But who may abide the day of his coming? and who shall stand when he appeareth? for he is like a refiner's fire, and like fullers' soap: (Malachi 3:1-2).

If the Bible discusses the second coming of Jesus, it has to mean that what follows is a New Testament event. I know it's written in the Old Testament, but it's a New Testament application. It has to be. This writing references events occurring before the second coming of Jesus, which would have to be after He ascended. It happens between His ascension and His second coming, which would be precisely in the time period we are in today.

We want to skip down a few verses:

> Will a man rob God? Yet ye have robbed me. But ye say, Wherein have we robbed thee? In tithes and offerings. Ye are cursed with a curse: for ye have robbed me, even this whole nation. Bring ye all the tithes into the storehouse, that there may be meat in mine house, and prove me now herewith, saith the Lord of hosts, if I will not open you the windows of heaven, and pour you out a blessing, that there shall not be room enough to receive it (Malachi 3:8-10).

Accordingly, we are to bring the tithe to the storehouse so there will be meat in His house. You could say it this way, *"That there may be dough in mine house."* It wouldn't be a violation because He already said to bring the dough in Ezekiel 44. That's a little play on words, but it fits. Now, I want you to pay close attention to this: The goal in your giving is **not** so you can get more stuff. The purpose of your giving is **to expand the kingdom of God.**

> Your goal in giving is not so you can get more stuff. Your goal in giving is to expand the kingdom of God.

There's always someone who says, *"The church just wants your money. The church just wants to be rich."* Well, what does "meat in mine house" mean? Your goal in giving is not so you can get more stuff. Your goal giving is to expand the kingdom of God.

Often, when we sow seed, we forget what we're doing. We sow seeds believing for our harvest. Should you believe for a harvest? Absolutely. Should you name your seed? Sure. Should you believe for God to do something for you? Yes. However, your priority is not your harvest. **Your priority is the house of the Lord.** You give to God. Then, He does His part back to you. We give to expand the kingdom of God. **The goal in your giving is to see God's house prosper and see God's house blessed.**

Now, what did we read in Malachi? It said, "That there may be meat in mine house." That's the goal of your giving. The objective in your giving is **not** that there may be meat in **your** house. I'm emphasizing this because sometimes we can give with greedy motives. It's important to give with the right heart when you lay your offering on the altar. If you begrudge the church of the Living God prospering, you will never be out of debt. We must get the church out of debt in order to get ourselves out of debt. The principle is to put the dough in the house of God so that blessing might rest on your house.

The Bible says in Malachi that when you bring the tithe into God's house, He will open the windows of heaven to you. Again, the goal is **not** to get the windows of heaven open. The goal is to put meat in His house, and the byproduct is you living under an open heaven. God wants you under an open heaven. However, the goal is to prosper the kingdom of God.

You can find something interesting in the book of 1 Timothy:

> But if I tarry long, that thou mayest know how thou oughtest to behave thyself in the **house** of God, which is the **church** of the living God, the pillar and ground of the truth (1 Timothy 3:15, emphasis added).

According to this verse, the house of God is the church of God. So, we bring our gift to the altar in the house of God. We present it to God from our hearts. If we have an ought against any, we rid ourselves of the encumbrances. We deal with our motives. The God of heaven is the God of the temple, who is also the God of the altar. The gift is not the sacred thing, but the gift becomes sacred because it was presented on the altar. It wasn't sacred when it was at your house. It wasn't sacred when it was lying in the yard. It wasn't sacred when it was lying out on the street.

I went to the movies the other day, and there was $20 lying on the ground with no one around. That $20 bill lying there on that sidewalk is not sanctified money. It's just money. What did I do? I picked it up, and when I got home, I placed it in this particular tray where I always lay my tithe. Now, it's sanctified because I set it apart for the kingdom of God, and when I come back to church on the first day of the week, I will give it as God has prospered me. Someone could be thinking, *"Well, that money just showed up. You don't have to tithe on that."* You don't have to, but I do it. Even when I get a Christmas gift or birthday present, I don't always know the value, so I try to estimate. I tithe on all of it. This is just part of our life, and God has blessed us beyond measure. The blessing rests in our house.

The point is that we ought to know how to behave in the house of God, which is the church of God. That's what this Scripture in 1 Timothy says. So, when the Bible tells us to bring all the tithe into the storehouse, He's talking about bringing **all** the tithe to the church. We do it God's way. Then, as we prioritize God's house with our giving, with our gifts, He positions us for supernatural debt reduction. However, if your motive is, *"I'm going to give to the church so I can get out of debt supernaturally,"* it won't work. You give to the church to bless the church, and God will get you out of debt. It's the same process, but it's not the same thought process.

## A FINAL WORD

So, we should love what God loves and hate what God hates. If God loves the lost, we love the lost. If God loves the church, we love the church. Therefore, we tithe. We bring our gifts and our offerings to the Lord. When you bless God's house, the Bible says God will let the blessing rest in your house. You are positioned now to receive.

I don't know how He will do it for you because God uniquely deals with each of us. You are not just one of the masses; you are a totally unique individual with different life circumstances and needs, and God will deal with you on a personal basis. But, without a shadow of a doubt, He will get it to you. Believe God's prophets; believe what they say, and He will get it to you. Another person can't get it to you, but God can get it to you, and He will!

Think about this verse as you read it. It says:

> "For the sake of the house of the LORD our God, I will seek your prosperity" (Psalm 122:9, NIV).

This verse says that our entire motive in prospering should be for the sake of God's house. Someone says, *"Well, I don't want to prosper."* It's selfish to withhold prosperity from God's house because it prospers as you prosper. We don't live this life unto ourselves. We are to be what God called and created us to be. You ought to live in the abundance He called you to live in. You should want to live above the dregs of this planet. Why? I will seek prosperity "for the sake of the house of the Lord."

Prosper on purpose. We should prosper because we're supposed to prosper. God expects it of me, and He expects it of you. He wants it for you while you remember the goal is not your prosperity.

Make this your confession and believe it:

> *I will seek prosperity for the house of the Lord. I will make the house of the Lord prosperous, and God will see to mine. I'll make the house of the Lord prosperous, and God will take care of me.*

# About the Author

**Dr. Ed King** is the founder and Senior Pastor of Redemption Church in Knoxville, Tennessee. He also serves as the president of "The Power of the Word" television ministry, which broadcasts to both national and international markets. In addition to these duties, Dr. King has authored ten books to date and traveled to over 60 nations around the world—teaching and preaching the gospel to thousands of people in leadership conferences and evangelistic meetings. He makes his home in Knoxville with his wife and co-Pastor, Nora King. Together they have a daughter, Laren, and son, Marcus, who is in heaven.

Power of the Word Ministries
Dr. Ed King
PO Box 52466
Knoxville TN 37950 USA
1.800.956.4433
www.poweroftheword.com
info@poweroftheword.com
youtube.com/user/RedemptionChurch

Redemption Church
3550 Pleasant Ridge Rd
Knoxville TN 37921 USA
865.521.7777
www.redemptionchurch.com
info@redemptionchurch.com
youtube.com/user/RedemptionChurch

# BOOKS BY DR. ED KING

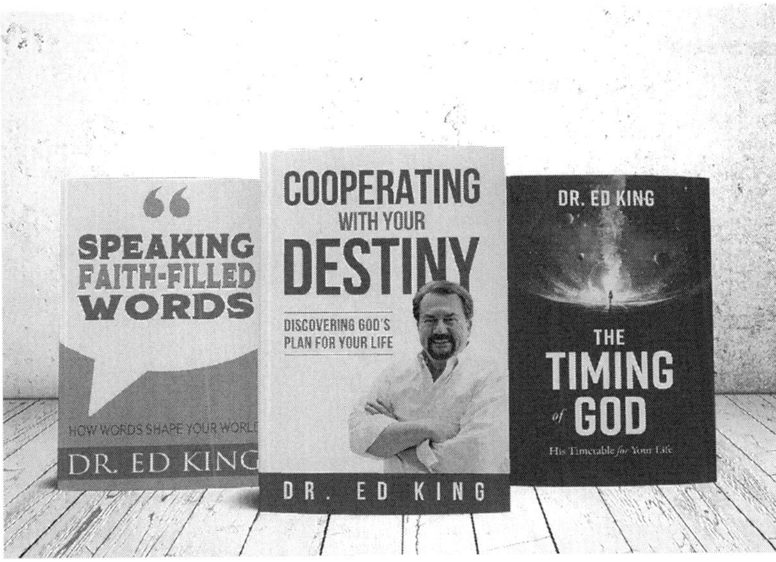


SPEAKING FAIHTH-FILLED WORDS
ISBN: 9781602731486 • 162 pages.

COOPERATING WITH YOUR DESTINY
ISBN: 9781602731349 • 232 pages.

THE TIMING OF GOD—His Timetable for Your Life
ISBN: 9781602730717 • 118 pages.

WHAT'S GOING ON?
Why I Believe We Are the Rapture Generation
ISBN: 9781973638872 • 298 pages • Westbow Press

# BOOKS BY DR. ED KING

## SUPERNATURAL PROVISION—Uncovering the Mystery of God's Blessing

Is it possible today to live in God's blessing? Yes, when we obey the Lord's highest command: SEEK HIM FIRST. Learn how to seek God first from a heart of love and devotion. Then, when doing the work of the Kingdom, He will generate a supernatural flow of provision to distinguish you from the world. Veteran author Dr. Ed King concludes by issuing a charge to embrace the sacredness of God's blessing as a reward to those who seek Him first.
ISBN: 9781602731547 • 254 pages • Parsons Publishing House

## SPEAKING FAITH-FILLED Words—How Words Shape Your World

Everyone wants to enjoy life and be satisfied! Having a good life is not about wealth or entitlement but about connecting with God, operating in faith, and living in His promises. Veteran author, Dr. Ed King, tells you how to embrace God's promises through speaking faith-filled words. It's time to engage God with your burning faith and release your words to shape your world
ISBN: 9781602731486 • 160 pages • Parsons Publishing House

## LOYALTY—Going Beyond Faithfulness

Pastor Ed King elaborates on the distinctions between faithfulness and loyalty and focuses on lessons learned by looking at the brotherly love of Jonathan and David. Learn how God's grace will meet you to go past faithfulness and enter into loyalty. It all starts with a decision!
ISBN: 9781602730793 • 110 pages • Parsons Publishing House

## WILL MY PET BE IN HEAVEN?

In this book, Pastor Ed King gives us a solid, biblical answer about your pet's afterlife. If you or someone you know has lost a pet, you will find great comfort and insight into what the Bible has to say about our beloved animals and their future in heaven.
ISBN: 9781602730687 • 92 pages • Parsons Publishing House

# BOOKS BY DR. ED KING

## COOPERATING WITH YOUR DESTINY—Discovering God's Plan for Your Life

Seeking God's purpose for your life—what He put you on this planet to do—is the most important thing you could ever pursue! God has a good plan for your life that has been designed just for you. Your destiny is a partnership with God orchestrated to cause you to flourish and obtain your eternal reward—all you have to do is join with God's plan!
ISBN: 9781602731349 • 232 pages • Parsons Publishing House

## DEDICATING YOUR HOUSE

Dedicating your house is a rite that every Christian should perform in order to live a quiet and peaceful life. Because you live in your house, you should want and expect God's blessings on it. One way to see those blessings is to thoughtfully and sacredly separate your house for the Lord's work and service. In this book, Dr. King lays out the biblical case for dedicating your house and provides eight easy-to-follow steps.
ISBN: 9781602730861 • 114 pages • Parsons Publishing House

## THE TIMING OF GOD—His Timetable for Your Life

In this life–changing book, you will discover the true timetable that God has set up for you at creation. You will see everything in life has a time and a season. God wants to give you remarkable things to experience, but He wants to give them to you when you are ready to handle and enjoy them. After reading and studying this book, you will become more assured than ever that your next move will be by the inspiration and the timing of God.
ISBN: 9781602730717 • 118 pages • Parsons Publishing House

## WHAT'S GOING ON?—Why I Believe We Are the Rapture Generation

Although the Bible tells us that no one knows the day or the hour of Jesus' return, God's Word does reveal solid information that illustrates how the signs of the times are lining up for His return to the earth. Pastor Ed King shares insight about the many signs appearing and circumstances playing out at this very hour. ISBN: 9781973638872 • 298 pages • Westbow Press